Raymond Kurzweil

The AI Visionary's Untold Story – Unauthorized

Arjun Ahmed

ISBN: 9781779699855
Imprint: Telephasic Workshop
Copyright © 2024 Arjun Ahmed.
All Rights Reserved.

Contents

Prologue: The Mind of a Visionary   **1**
The Early Years   1
The Path to Success   8
The Kurzweil Reading Machine   15
The Singularity is Near   21
The Art of Transcendence   41

Chapter Two: A Futuristic Mind   **57**
A Visionary Thinker   57
The Age of Intelligent Machines   65
The Virtual Cosmos   72
Adventures in Health and Longevity   79
The Future of Education   85

Chapter Three: The Genius Unleashed   **93**
Innovations in Speech Recognition   93
The Quest for Strong AI   100
The New Mind   107
Music, Art, and Creativity   115

Bibliography   **119**
The Legacy Continues   123

Index   **131**

Prologue: The Mind of a Visionary

The Early Years

A Curious Child

Raymond Kurzweil's journey into the world of technology and artificial intelligence began in the vibrant tapestry of his childhood. Born in 1948, in the bustling city of New York, Kurzweil exhibited an insatiable curiosity from a young age. This curiosity was not merely a fleeting interest; it was a profound drive that would shape his future endeavors and innovations.

Early Interests

As a child, Kurzweil was fascinated by the mechanics of the world around him. He often disassembled household appliances, eager to understand their inner workings. This hands-on approach was pivotal in nurturing his analytical skills. He once recalled taking apart his mother's radio, only to find himself overwhelmed by the complexity of its components. Yet, rather than deterring him, this experience ignited a passion for understanding machines at a deeper level.

Kurzweil's early interests were not limited to machines alone. He was also drawn to the world of music. The harmonious blend of creativity and technology became apparent as he began playing the saxophone at the age of five. This duality of interests—music and machinery—would later converge in his groundbreaking work in artificial intelligence and creativity.

Inspiration from Family

Family played a crucial role in shaping Kurzweil's inquisitive nature. His father, a musician and a teacher, instilled in him a love for learning and exploration. Kurzweil's mother, a strong-willed woman, encouraged him to pursue his interests relentlessly. They fostered an environment where questioning the status quo was not only welcomed but celebrated. This nurturing atmosphere allowed Kurzweil to flourish, as he often engaged in discussions about science and technology with his family.

First Encounters with Computers

The pivotal moment in Kurzweil's early life came when he was introduced to computers. At the age of 13, he attended a summer camp where he was first exposed to programming. The experience was transformative; he found himself captivated by the idea of creating something from scratch. It was here that he learned to program on a primitive computer, which, at the time, was a novel concept for most people.

Kurzweil often reminisced about writing his first program, a simple game that involved guessing a number. The thrill of seeing the machine respond to his commands was exhilarating. This encounter solidified his desire to delve deeper into the world of computing, setting the stage for a lifetime of exploration and innovation.

A Mind Like No Other

Kurzweil's curiosity was not confined to the tangible aspects of technology. He was also deeply interested in the philosophical implications of machines and intelligence. He often pondered questions such as:

$$\text{What defines intelligence?} \tag{1}$$

This inquiry led him to explore various fields, including cognitive science and neuroscience, as he sought to understand the nature of human thought and its potential replication in machines.

His voracious reading habits further fueled his intellectual pursuits. Kurzweil devoured books on mathematics, science fiction, and philosophy, often finding inspiration in the works of visionaries like Isaac Asimov and Arthur C. Clarke. These literary influences not only shaped his understanding of technology but also inspired him to envision a future where machines could augment human capabilities.

A Visionary's Foundation

In hindsight, Kurzweil's childhood was marked by a unique blend of curiosity, creativity, and intellect. The experiences and influences during these formative years laid a strong foundation for his later achievements. His early fascination with machines and the philosophical questions surrounding them would ultimately lead him to become one of the most influential figures in the field of artificial intelligence.

Kurzweil's journey from a curious child to a pioneering innovator exemplifies the profound impact of nurturing one's innate interests. His story serves as a reminder that curiosity, when combined with passion and perseverance, can lead to extraordinary discoveries and advancements in technology.

In conclusion, the seeds of innovation were sown early in Kurzweil's life. The curious child who disassembled radios and wrote simple programs would grow into a visionary who would challenge the boundaries of what machines could achieve. As we delve deeper into his life and contributions, it becomes clear that the curiosity that defined his childhood was merely the beginning of a remarkable journey into the future of technology.

Lifelong Fascination with Machines

From a tender age, Raymond Kurzweil exhibited an insatiable curiosity about the workings of machines. This fascination would lay the groundwork for a career that would not only redefine technology but also challenge the very fabric of human existence. His childhood was punctuated by a series of exploratory endeavors that reflected a mind constantly engaged with the mechanics of the world around him.

Kurzweil's early interactions with machines were not merely playful; they were deeply analytical. He often dismantled household appliances, driven by a desire to understand their inner workings. This hands-on approach is reminiscent of the constructivist learning theory proposed by Jean Piaget, which posits that knowledge is constructed through interaction with the environment. Kurzweil's explorations can be viewed as a practical application of this theory, wherein he actively engaged with the physical world to form a mental model of how machines operate.

$$\text{Knowledge} = f(\text{Experience}) \tag{2}$$

In this equation, Knowledge is a function of Experience, illustrating that Kurzweil's understanding of machines was directly proportional to his hands-on experiences. For instance, at the age of just five, he was already fascinated by the mechanics of his father's radio. He would spend hours tuning in to different frequencies, captivated by the idea that invisible waves could carry sound across vast distances. This early experience not only sparked his interest in communication technologies but also laid the foundation for his later work in artificial intelligence and machine learning.

As he grew older, Kurzweil's fascination evolved into more complex projects. He built his first computer from scratch at the age of 15, a feat that would astound many of his peers. This endeavor was not just a technical challenge; it was an embodiment of his belief in the potential of machines to enhance human capabilities. The computer he constructed was a simple yet elegant design, showcasing his understanding of both hardware and software. This early project was a precursor to his later innovations in machine learning and artificial intelligence.

Kurzweil's journey into the realm of machines was also influenced by the theoretical frameworks of cybernetics, a field that explores the regulatory systems of machines and living beings. Norbert Wiener, the father of cybernetics, argued that machines could learn and adapt through feedback loops. Kurzweil embraced this concept, believing that the interplay between human intelligence and machine intelligence could lead to unprecedented advancements.

$$\text{Feedback Loop} = \text{Input} \rightarrow \text{Process} \rightarrow \text{Output} \rightarrow \text{Feedback} \qquad (3)$$

In this feedback loop, the Input is the data received by the machine, which is then processed to produce an Output. The Feedback from the output can then be used to refine the input, creating a cycle of continuous improvement. This principle became a guiding philosophy for Kurzweil as he ventured into developing technologies that would eventually revolutionize the fields of artificial intelligence and machine learning.

Kurzweil's fascination with machines also led him to explore the concept of exponential growth in technology, a principle he famously articulated in his later works. He observed that the capabilities of machines were not merely improving linearly but were instead following an exponential curve. This observation can be mathematically represented as:

$$T(n) = T_0 \cdot 2^{\frac{n}{d}} \qquad (4)$$

Where $T(n)$ represents the technology's capability at time n, T_0 is the initial capability, and d is the doubling time. This equation encapsulates Kurzweil's belief that as technology advances, the potential for machines to augment human life increases exponentially.

THE EARLY YEARS 5

In conclusion, Raymond Kurzweil's lifelong fascination with machines was not merely a hobby; it was a profound engagement with the possibilities of technology. His early experiences shaped his understanding of the intricate relationship between humans and machines, laying the groundwork for a career marked by groundbreaking innovations. As he moved forward in life, this initial curiosity would evolve into a visionary quest to merge human intelligence with artificial intelligence, ultimately leading to his profound contributions to the fields of technology and beyond.

Building His First Computer

In the early 1970s, a young Raymond Kurzweil found himself captivated by the idea of creating a machine that could think. This fascination, coupled with a natural curiosity, led him down the path of building his first computer—a pivotal moment that would shape his future endeavors and set the stage for his groundbreaking contributions to technology.

The Genesis of a Computer

Kurzweil's journey began with a simple yet profound realization: a computer was essentially a machine that processed information. To him, the essence of computing could be distilled into the manipulation of binary data, where each bit represented a state of either 0 or 1. This binary system is foundational in computer science, as it allows for the representation of complex data structures and operations.

The construction of his first computer was not merely an academic exercise; it was a hands-on exploration of the principles of electronics and programming. Kurzweil started with basic components: resistors, capacitors, and transistors, which he carefully assembled to create a rudimentary circuit. The circuit served as the backbone of his computer, allowing him to understand how electronic signals could be harnessed to perform calculations.

Understanding the Components

Kurzweil's first computer was built using the following key components:

- **Transistors:** These semiconductor devices acted as electronic switches, controlling the flow of electricity in the circuit. By combining multiple transistors, Kurzweil could create logic gates, the building blocks of digital circuits.

- **Resistors and Capacitors:** Resistors limited the flow of current, while capacitors stored electrical energy. Together, they formed the basic circuits necessary for timing and signal processing.

- **A Breadboard:** This tool allowed Kurzweil to prototype his design without soldering, enabling him to experiment with different configurations and troubleshoot issues easily.

The foundational equation governing the behavior of these components is Ohm's Law, which is expressed as:

$$V = I \times R \qquad (5)$$

where V is the voltage across the resistor, I is the current flowing through it, and R is the resistance. Understanding this relationship was crucial for Kurzweil as he designed circuits that would eventually execute simple programs.

Programming the Machine

Once the hardware was assembled, Kurzweil turned his attention to programming. He began with a low-level programming language that allowed him to directly manipulate the machine's hardware. This experience was critical, as it provided him with insights into how software interacts with hardware—a concept that remains central to computer science today.

Kurzweil wrote simple algorithms to perform arithmetic operations, such as addition and subtraction, using binary arithmetic. The binary addition operation can be represented as follows:

$$\text{Sum} = A + B \qquad (6)$$

where A and B are binary numbers. The process of carrying over bits during addition was a challenge that required careful attention to detail, but it was also a thrilling puzzle that deepened his understanding of computational logic.

Challenges Faced

Building his first computer was not without its challenges. Kurzweil encountered several problems, including:

- **Component Limitations:** Access to high-quality components was limited, which sometimes resulted in unreliable circuits. He learned to troubleshoot and replace faulty parts, honing his problem-solving skills.

- **Programming Bugs:** Debugging was a tedious process, often requiring him to meticulously check each line of code and circuit connection. This experience taught him the importance of precision in programming.

- **Understanding Logic:** As he delved deeper into the world of logic gates and circuits, he grappled with the abstract concepts of Boolean algebra, which underpins digital logic design.

Despite these hurdles, Kurzweil's determination fueled his progress. He would often spend hours immersed in his work, driven by an insatiable curiosity and a desire to understand the inner workings of his creation.

The Impact of the Experience

The experience of building his first computer was transformative for Kurzweil. It instilled in him a belief that technology could be harnessed to enhance human capabilities. He began to envision a future where machines could not only assist humans but also augment their intelligence and creativity.

This early foray into computing laid the groundwork for Kurzweil's later innovations. It was a formative experience that shaped his philosophy regarding the interplay between humanity and technology. As he would later articulate, the potential of artificial intelligence was not merely a technical challenge but a profound opportunity to redefine what it means to be human.

In retrospect, building that first computer was more than just a project; it was a declaration of his intent to push the boundaries of what technology could achieve. It was the beginning of a lifelong journey that would lead him to become one of the most influential figures in the field of artificial intelligence.

Conclusion

Raymond Kurzweil's adventure in building his first computer was a microcosm of his larger vision. It encapsulated the spirit of innovation and exploration that would define his career. As he moved forward, the lessons learned during this formative period would resonate throughout his life, guiding his contributions to technology, AI, and the ongoing quest for understanding the very nature of consciousness.

The Path to Success

Early Entrepreneurial Ventures

Raymond Kurzweil's journey into the world of entrepreneurship began at a remarkably young age, fueled by an insatiable curiosity and a knack for innovation. His early ventures were not merely attempts to make money; they were reflections of his deep-seated passion for technology and a desire to solve real-world problems.

The First Venture: The Kurzweil Music System

At the tender age of 15, Kurzweil started his first entrepreneurial endeavor, the Kurzweil Music System, which combined his love for music with his burgeoning technical skills. He developed a synthesizer that could replicate the sounds of various musical instruments. This was not just a simple electronic device; it was a groundbreaking product that paved the way for future innovations in music technology.

The Kurzweil Music System utilized a technique known as *waveform sampling*, which involved recording the sound of an instrument and digitally reproducing it. This method can be expressed mathematically as:

$$S(t) = \sum_{n=0}^{N} A_n \cdot \sin(2\pi f_n t + \phi_n) \qquad (7)$$

where $S(t)$ is the sound wave at time t, A_n represents the amplitude of each harmonic, f_n is the frequency, and ϕ_n is the phase shift. This synthesis technique allowed musicians to create complex soundscapes that were previously unattainable with conventional instruments.

The Challenge of Market Acceptance

Despite the innovative nature of the Kurzweil Music System, Kurzweil faced significant challenges in gaining market acceptance. The music industry was hesitant to embrace digital technology, fearing it would undermine traditional music creation. Kurzweil's perseverance paid off when he secured a contract with the renowned musician Stevie Wonder, who used the synthesizer in his performances. This endorsement not only validated Kurzweil's invention but also opened doors for further collaborations and sales.

The Birth of Kurzweil Computer Products

Following the success of his music system, Kurzweil founded Kurzweil Computer Products in 1972. His vision was to create technologies that could enhance human capabilities. The company initially focused on developing products that combined optical character recognition (OCR) with speech synthesis. This venture was driven by Kurzweil's belief that technology could empower individuals with disabilities, allowing them to access information that was previously out of reach.

Optical Character Recognition: A Revolutionary Leap

Kurzweil's OCR technology was revolutionary. It enabled machines to read text aloud, transforming the way visually impaired individuals interacted with printed materials. The underlying principle of OCR can be described using the following function:

$$R(x,y) = \int_{-\infty}^{\infty} f(t) \cdot g(t-x)\, dt \tag{8}$$

where $R(x,y)$ is the resulting image, $f(t)$ represents the input image, and $g(t)$ is the recognition function. This technology not only showcased Kurzweil's technical prowess but also his commitment to social impact.

The Impact on Accessibility

The introduction of Kurzweil's OCR technology marked a turning point in accessibility. It allowed visually impaired individuals to read books, newspapers, and other printed materials independently. The impact was profound, as it opened up new avenues for education and employment for people with disabilities. Kurzweil's ability to identify a gap in the market and create a solution exemplifies the essence of entrepreneurship.

Lessons Learned and Future Aspirations

Through these early ventures, Kurzweil learned several critical lessons about entrepreneurship. First, he recognized the importance of resilience in the face of skepticism. Second, he understood that innovation must be paired with a genuine understanding of user needs. Finally, he appreciated the value of collaboration, as partnerships with artists and other innovators propelled his ideas forward.

As Kurzweil continued to innovate, his entrepreneurial spirit remained undeterred. He was not just building businesses; he was laying the groundwork for a future where technology and humanity could coexist harmoniously.

In summary, Kurzweil's early entrepreneurial ventures laid the foundation for his later achievements. His ability to merge technology with a vision for social good set him apart as a pioneer in the field, inspiring countless others to follow in his footsteps. The lessons he learned during this formative period would shape his approach to innovation and entrepreneurship for decades to come.

Academic Pursuits and Achievements

Raymond Kurzweil's academic journey is a testament to his relentless curiosity and passion for technology. From a young age, he exhibited an insatiable thirst for knowledge, which laid the foundation for his future innovations. His academic pursuits were not just a means to an end; they were a vital part of his identity and a driving force behind his groundbreaking contributions to the fields of artificial intelligence and machine learning.

High School Years and Early Interests

Kurzweil attended the prestigious Newton North High School in Massachusetts, where he excelled in mathematics and science. His early exposure to computers during this period sparked a fascination that would shape his future. He was particularly drawn to the emerging field of computer science, which was still in its infancy during the 1960s. Kurzweil's high school projects included programming early computers, where he experimented with algorithms and learned the basics of coding.

Undergraduate Studies at MIT

After graduating from high school, Kurzweil enrolled at the Massachusetts Institute of Technology (MIT), one of the leading institutions in technology and engineering. At MIT, he pursued a degree in electrical engineering and computer science, which provided him with a solid foundation in both theoretical and practical aspects of technology.

During his time at MIT, Kurzweil was exposed to various cutting-edge technologies and theories that would later influence his work. He was particularly intrigued by the concept of artificial intelligence, which was gaining traction in academic circles. Under the mentorship of renowned professors, he delved into subjects such as neural networks and pattern recognition, which would become central themes in his later innovations.

Research Contributions

Kurzweil's academic achievements were not limited to coursework; he actively engaged in research that would have lasting implications in the field of artificial intelligence. His undergraduate thesis focused on the development of algorithms for optical character recognition (OCR), a technology that would revolutionize the way machines interpret text. This early research laid the groundwork for his later invention of the Kurzweil Reading Machine, which utilized OCR to assist visually impaired individuals.

The OCR algorithms he developed were based on the principles of pattern recognition, where the machine learns to identify characters by analyzing their shapes and structures. Mathematically, this can be represented as a function $f : X \rightarrow Y$, where X is the set of input patterns (characters) and Y is the set of recognized outputs. The goal of the algorithm is to minimize the error in recognition, expressed as:

$$E = \sum_{i=1}^{n}(y_i - f(x_i))^2$$

where E is the error, y_i is the actual output, and $f(x_i)$ is the predicted output.

Graduate Studies and Further Exploration

After completing his undergraduate degree, Kurzweil continued his studies at MIT, pursuing a master's degree. His graduate research focused on speech recognition technology, another area that captivated his interest. He explored the complexities of human speech patterns and sought to create machines that could understand and process natural language.

One of the significant challenges in speech recognition is the variability of human speech, which can be influenced by factors such as accent, tone, and speed. Kurzweil's work in this area involved developing statistical models that could adapt to these variations. He applied techniques from information theory to enhance the accuracy of speech recognition systems, which can be mathematically represented using concepts such as entropy $H(X)$:

$$H(X) = -\sum_{i=1}^{n} p(x_i) \log p(x_i)$$

where $p(x_i)$ is the probability of occurrence of the speech pattern x_i.

Awards and Recognition

Kurzweil's academic achievements did not go unnoticed. He received numerous accolades during his time at MIT, including scholarships and awards for his innovative research. His contributions to the field of artificial intelligence were recognized by his peers, and he was invited to present his findings at various conferences and symposiums.

In addition to his academic accolades, Kurzweil's work laid the foundation for future advancements in artificial intelligence and machine learning. His early research in OCR and speech recognition paved the way for technologies that are now integral to our daily lives, such as virtual assistants and automated transcription services.

Conclusion

Raymond Kurzweil's academic pursuits and achievements reflect a profound commitment to understanding and advancing technology. His time at MIT was marked by groundbreaking research that would shape the future of artificial intelligence. Through his dedication to learning and innovation, Kurzweil not only contributed to the academic community but also set the stage for a lifetime of transformative inventions. His journey from a curious student to a pioneering technologist exemplifies the power of education and the impact one individual can have on the world.

Founding Kurzweil Computer Products

In the early 1970s, Raymond Kurzweil embarked on a journey that would forever alter the landscape of technology and accessibility. Fueled by his insatiable curiosity and a deep-seated desire to create machines that could enhance human capabilities, he founded Kurzweil Computer Products in 1972. This venture was not merely a business; it was the manifestation of Kurzweil's vision to bridge the gap between technology and the human experience.

At the core of Kurzweil's entrepreneurial spirit was the belief that technology could serve a greater purpose. He was motivated by a desire to make a difference in the lives of those who were often overlooked by mainstream technology. This led him to focus on developing products that could assist the visually impaired. The first significant breakthrough came with the creation of the Kurzweil Reading

Machine, an invention that would revolutionize the way blind individuals interacted with printed text.

The Vision Behind the Company

Kurzweil's vision was rooted in the principles of artificial intelligence and machine learning. He sought to create machines that could understand human language and interpret visual information. The challenge was immense: how could a machine be taught to read, comprehend, and vocalize text? This question became the cornerstone of his work at Kurzweil Computer Products.

To tackle this challenge, Kurzweil assembled a team of talented engineers and researchers. They utilized cutting-edge techniques in optical character recognition (OCR) and speech synthesis. The OCR technology allowed the machine to scan printed text, while the speech synthesis component transformed the scanned text into spoken words.

The theoretical framework behind OCR can be described by the following equation:

$$\text{OCR}(I) = \sum_{i=1}^{n} f(i) \cdot P(i) \tag{9}$$

Where: - I represents the input image containing printed text. - $f(i)$ is a function that identifies and segments individual characters in the image. - $P(i)$ is the probability of each character being correctly recognized.

The team faced numerous problems during the development phase, including the need to improve the accuracy of character recognition and the naturalness of the synthesized speech. Early prototypes often struggled with complex fonts, varying text sizes, and the nuances of human speech patterns.

The Breakthrough: Kurzweil Reading Machine

The culmination of their efforts was the Kurzweil Reading Machine, launched in 1976. This groundbreaking device was the first to successfully read printed text aloud, and it was met with widespread acclaim. The Reading Machine used a combination of OCR and speech synthesis technologies, allowing it to read a variety of materials, from books to newspapers.

The impact of the Kurzweil Reading Machine on the visually impaired community was profound. For the first time, individuals who were blind or had severe visual impairments could access written information independently. This innovation not only enhanced their quality of life but also empowered them to participate more fully in society.

Kurzweil's work did not go unnoticed. The Reading Machine garnered numerous awards, including accolades from organizations dedicated to advancing technology for individuals with disabilities. It became a symbol of what could be achieved when technology was harnessed for the greater good.

Challenges and Innovations

Despite the initial success, Kurzweil Computer Products faced significant challenges. The costs associated with producing the Reading Machine were high, and the market for such specialized technology was limited. However, Kurzweil's determination to make his products accessible led to innovative solutions.

He sought partnerships with nonprofit organizations and government agencies to subsidize costs and expand distribution. This approach not only made the Reading Machine more affordable but also raised awareness about the capabilities of assistive technology.

Furthermore, Kurzweil continued to innovate. He introduced enhancements to the Reading Machine, including improved OCR algorithms and more natural-sounding speech synthesis. These advancements were grounded in ongoing research in artificial intelligence, reflecting Kurzweil's commitment to staying at the forefront of technological progress.

Legacy of Kurzweil Computer Products

The founding of Kurzweil Computer Products marked a pivotal moment in the intersection of technology and accessibility. Kurzweil's vision laid the groundwork for future innovations in assistive technology, inspiring a generation of entrepreneurs and engineers to pursue similar paths.

The legacy of the Kurzweil Reading Machine lives on in modern technologies that continue to break barriers for individuals with disabilities. Today, advancements in artificial intelligence and machine learning have led to even more sophisticated tools that enhance accessibility, proving that Kurzweil's original vision was not just a dream, but a catalyst for change.

In conclusion, the founding of Kurzweil Computer Products was not merely an entrepreneurial endeavor; it was a testament to the power of innovation driven by compassion. Raymond Kurzweil's journey exemplifies how one person's vision can change the world, making technology a force for good in the lives of countless individuals.

The Kurzweil Reading Machine

The Inspiration behind the Invention

Raymond Kurzweil's journey towards inventing the Kurzweil Reading Machine was not merely a product of scientific inquiry but a deeply personal quest fueled by empathy and a profound understanding of human limitations. The spark that ignited this monumental endeavor can be traced back to Kurzweil's childhood experiences and his interactions with individuals facing challenges that many take for granted.

Kurzweil's early exposure to technology and machines, combined with his innate curiosity, laid the groundwork for his future innovations. However, it was the realization that technology could serve a greater purpose—specifically, to enhance the lives of those with disabilities—that became the cornerstone of his vision. The inspiration for the Reading Machine emerged from a poignant moment in his life: a visit to a local school for the blind. Witnessing the struggles of students who were unable to access printed material, Kurzweil was struck by the profound barriers that limited their educational opportunities and social engagement.

> "Technology should be a bridge, not a barrier," Kurzweil often reflected, emphasizing the need for inclusive solutions.

This encounter ignited a passion within him to create a device that could convert printed text into speech, effectively breaking down the walls of isolation faced by the visually impaired. Kurzweil's vision was not only to invent a machine but to give a voice to those who had been silenced by circumstance.

The theoretical foundation for the Kurzweil Reading Machine was rooted in the principles of Optical Character Recognition (OCR). The ability to convert images of text into machine-encoded text was a significant leap forward in making information accessible. The challenge lay in developing an algorithm capable of recognizing various fonts, sizes, and styles of printed text, which was a formidable task in the early 1970s.

To illustrate the complexities involved, consider the mathematical formulation of OCR, which can be represented as a function f that maps images I to textual representations T:

$$f : I \to T$$

Where: - I represents the input image containing text, - T denotes the output textual data.

The function f relies on several sub-processes including image preprocessing, feature extraction, and classification. Each of these processes must be finely tuned to handle the variances in text presentation. For instance, image preprocessing often involves techniques such as binarization, where the image is converted to a binary format to simplify the data:

$$I_{binary}(x, y) = \begin{cases} 1 & \text{if } I(x, y) > \text{threshold} \\ 0 & \text{otherwise} \end{cases}$$

Where (x, y) are the pixel coordinates of the image I.

Kurzweil's innovative approach to OCR involved the use of neural networks, a concept that was still in its infancy at the time. By training these networks to recognize patterns in the data, he was able to significantly improve the accuracy of text recognition. This methodology not only addressed the immediate needs of the visually impaired but also laid the groundwork for future advancements in artificial intelligence.

The breakthrough came in 1976 when Kurzweil successfully demonstrated his Reading Machine at a conference, instantly capturing the attention of educators, technologists, and advocates for the disabled. The machine was capable of reading aloud printed text with impressive clarity and speed, transforming the lives of countless individuals.

Moreover, Kurzweil's invention was not just a technical achievement; it was a testament to the power of empathy-driven innovation. He often recounted stories of users who had regained their independence and confidence through the use of his technology. One particularly moving account involved a blind student who, for the first time, could read books on his own, igniting a passion for literature that had previously been out of reach.

In conclusion, the inspiration behind the Kurzweil Reading Machine was a confluence of personal experiences, theoretical exploration, and a commitment to harnessing technology for social good. Kurzweil's vision transcended the mere act of invention; it was about creating a future where barriers to knowledge and communication were dismantled, allowing every individual to participate fully in society. This ethos would continue to guide Kurzweil in his subsequent endeavors, establishing him as a true pioneer in the field of artificial intelligence and accessibility.

Breakthroughs and Innovations

Raymond Kurzweil's journey into the world of technology and innovation is marked by a series of groundbreaking achievements that have not only transformed industries but also redefined the relationship between humans and machines. One of his most significant contributions is the development of the Kurzweil Reading Machine, which emerged from his commitment to making information accessible to the visually impaired community.

The Concept of Optical Character Recognition (OCR)

At the heart of the Kurzweil Reading Machine lies the concept of Optical Character Recognition (OCR). OCR technology enables computers to recognize printed or handwritten text and convert it into machine-readable format. This innovation was revolutionary in the 1970s, as it provided a means for visually impaired individuals to access printed materials independently. The fundamental principle of OCR can be described mathematically as follows:

$$\text{Text}_{\text{output}} = f(\text{Image}_{\text{input}}) \tag{10}$$

Where f represents the OCR algorithm that processes the input image to produce an output text. Kurzweil's algorithm utilized a combination of pattern recognition and artificial intelligence techniques, enabling the machine to learn and adapt to different fonts and handwriting styles.

Breakthrough Innovations in OCR

Kurzweil's innovations in OCR were characterized by several key breakthroughs:

- **Multi-font Recognition:** Traditional OCR systems struggled with variations in font styles and sizes. Kurzweil developed a system capable of recognizing multiple fonts, which greatly enhanced the machine's versatility. This was achieved through a training process where the system learned to identify and differentiate between various characters based on their pixel patterns.

- **Text-to-Speech (TTS) Integration:** The Kurzweil Reading Machine was not just an OCR device; it integrated TTS technology, allowing the converted text to be read aloud. This integration was a significant advancement, as it provided an auditory output that was essential for visually impaired users. The TTS system utilized advanced speech synthesis techniques, including concatenative synthesis, where recorded speech segments were combined to form coherent sentences.

- **Real-time Processing:** One of the challenges in developing the Kurzweil Reading Machine was achieving real-time processing of text. Kurzweil's innovations in hardware and algorithms allowed the machine to scan and read text at a pace that matched human reading speed, making it practical for everyday use. The system employed parallel processing techniques to enhance speed and efficiency.

Impact on the Visually Impaired Community

The impact of Kurzweil's breakthroughs in OCR and TTS technology on the visually impaired community cannot be overstated. Prior to the introduction of the Kurzweil Reading Machine, access to printed materials was severely limited for individuals with visual impairments. The ability to independently read books, newspapers, and other printed documents transformed the lives of many, promoting inclusion and empowerment.

For instance, consider the story of a visually impaired student who, with the help of the Kurzweil Reading Machine, was able to read textbooks for the first time. This access not only improved academic performance but also fostered a sense of independence and self-efficacy. The machine became a vital tool in educational settings, enabling students to participate fully in classroom activities.

Challenges and Future Directions

Despite the successes of the Kurzweil Reading Machine, several challenges remained. One of the primary issues was the accuracy of OCR in recognizing text under varying conditions, such as poor lighting or complex backgrounds. To address this, ongoing research has focused on improving the robustness of OCR algorithms through machine learning techniques, particularly deep learning, which has shown promise in enhancing recognition accuracy.

Additionally, as technology continues to evolve, the integration of AI and natural language processing (NLP) into reading machines presents exciting opportunities for further advancements. Future iterations of reading technology could leverage these innovations to provide more context-aware reading experiences, such as summarizing text or providing definitions for unfamiliar words.

Conclusion

In summary, Raymond Kurzweil's breakthroughs in OCR and TTS technology through the Kurzweil Reading Machine represent a significant milestone in the intersection of technology and accessibility. His innovations not only advanced the field of artificial intelligence but also played a crucial role in improving the quality of life for visually impaired individuals. As we look to the future, the legacy of these breakthroughs will continue to inspire new developments that push the boundaries of what is possible in assistive technology.

Impact on the Visually Impaired Community

The invention of the Kurzweil Reading Machine marked a significant turning point for the visually impaired community, offering unprecedented access to printed material. This device, which combined optical character recognition (OCR) with text-to-speech technology, became a beacon of hope for many who had previously faced insurmountable barriers to information.

The Need for Accessibility

Before the advent of the Kurzweil Reading Machine, individuals with visual impairments relied heavily on Braille and audio recordings for their reading needs. While these methods provided some level of accessibility, they were limited in scope and availability. Braille, for instance, requires specialized training and can only convey a fraction of the printed materials available. Audio recordings, though beneficial, often lagged behind in terms of timely access to current literature, newspapers, and educational resources.

The gap in accessible information created a significant barrier, leading to a lack of awareness, education, and engagement with the broader world. This situation underscored the urgent need for innovative solutions that could bridge the divide between the sighted and visually impaired communities.

The Kurzweil Reading Machine: A Breakthrough

Raymond Kurzweil's invention was revolutionary. By integrating OCR technology, the machine could scan printed text and convert it into spoken words in real time. This innovation not only democratized access to information but also empowered individuals with visual impairments to engage more fully with their environment.

The Kurzweil Reading Machine utilized complex algorithms to recognize characters and words, which were then synthesized into natural-sounding speech. The underlying mathematical model can be expressed as follows:

$$T(x) = \sum_{i=1}^{n} a_i \cdot f_i(x) \qquad (11)$$

where $T(x)$ represents the synthesized speech output, a_i are the coefficients for each feature $f_i(x)$ extracted from the scanned text, and n is the number of features considered. This equation illustrates how the machine processes various attributes of the text to produce coherent speech.

Real-World Applications and Success Stories

The impact of the Kurzweil Reading Machine on the visually impaired community can be illustrated through various real-world applications and success stories. Educational institutions began adopting the technology, enabling students with visual impairments to participate in mainstream classrooms alongside their sighted peers.

For instance, a blind student named Sarah, who struggled with traditional learning methods, found new hope with the Kurzweil Reading Machine. By using the device, she could independently access textbooks, research materials, and even participate in discussions, leveling the playing field in her educational journey.

Additionally, the machine's introduction in public libraries and community centers allowed visually impaired individuals to access a wealth of information previously out of reach. The ability to read newspapers, magazines, and books in real time transformed the way they interacted with society, fostering a greater sense of inclusion and independence.

Challenges and Limitations

Despite its groundbreaking nature, the Kurzweil Reading Machine was not without challenges. Early models were bulky, expensive, and required a learning curve for users unfamiliar with technology. Furthermore, the accuracy of OCR technology was sometimes hindered by factors such as poor print quality, unusual fonts, or complex layouts.

Moreover, while the machine significantly improved access to printed materials, it did not address the broader spectrum of accessibility issues faced by the visually impaired community. For example, the device could not assist with non-textual information, such as diagrams, images, or graphs, which are often crucial in educational and professional contexts.

The Legacy of the Kurzweil Reading Machine

The legacy of the Kurzweil Reading Machine extends beyond its immediate impact on the visually impaired community. It paved the way for further innovations in assistive technologies, inspiring a new generation of developers and researchers to explore ways to enhance accessibility.

As technology has advanced, newer iterations of reading machines and software applications have emerged, building on Kurzweil's foundational work. Today, smartphones and other portable devices equipped with OCR capabilities and text-to-speech functionality continue to empower visually impaired individuals, offering them even greater autonomy and access to information.

In conclusion, the Kurzweil Reading Machine not only transformed the landscape of accessibility for the visually impaired community but also ignited a movement towards inclusivity and innovation in assistive technology. Its impact resonates to this day, reminding us of the profound difference that visionary thinking can make in the lives of individuals facing challenges.

The Singularity is Near

Exploring the Concept of Technological Singularity

The concept of the Technological Singularity, popularized by thinkers such as Raymond Kurzweil, refers to a hypothetical point in the future when technological growth becomes uncontrollable and irreversible, resulting in unforeseeable changes to human civilization. This notion is rooted in the idea that the exponential growth of technology, particularly in artificial intelligence (AI), will lead to machines that surpass human intelligence, fundamentally altering the trajectory of human existence.

At its core, the Singularity is characterized by the notion of accelerating returns, a term coined by Kurzweil himself. This principle suggests that the rate of technological progress is not linear but exponential. According to Kurzweil, the growth of computing power follows Moore's Law, which posits that the number of transistors on a microchip doubles approximately every two years, leading to a corresponding increase in computational capability. This exponential growth can be represented mathematically as:

$$N(t) = N_0 \cdot 2^{\frac{t}{T}} \tag{12}$$

where $N(t)$ is the number of transistors at time t, N_0 is the initial number of transistors, and T is the doubling time (approximately 2 years).

As technology advances, Kurzweil argues that the boundaries between human and machine intelligence will blur. He predicts that once we achieve a level of AI that can improve its own algorithms and hardware autonomously, a feedback loop will emerge, propelling us into a realm of intelligence far beyond our current capabilities. This self-improving AI could lead to a rapid acceleration of technological advancement, culminating in the Singularity.

However, the concept of the Singularity is not without its challenges and criticisms. One significant problem is the unpredictability of such an event. While Kurzweil and others envision a utopian future where humans and machines coexist harmoniously, critics argue that we may face severe ethical dilemmas and existential risks. For instance, if AI systems surpass human intelligence, they could potentially operate beyond our control, leading to scenarios where human values and safety are compromised.

Moreover, the implications of the Singularity extend to various domains, including economics, healthcare, and even warfare. As machines become increasingly capable, the job market may experience significant disruptions. The automation of tasks traditionally performed by humans could lead to widespread unemployment, necessitating a reevaluation of economic structures and social safety nets. The equation for the impact on jobs can be framed as:

$$J(t) = J_0 - A(t) \tag{13}$$

where $J(t)$ represents the number of jobs at time t, J_0 is the initial number of jobs, and $A(t)$ is the number of jobs automated by AI at time t.

In addition to economic challenges, ethical considerations regarding AI's role in society become paramount. Questions arise about the moral status of superintelligent machines and the extent to which they should be granted rights or responsibilities. The potential for bias in AI algorithms also poses a significant risk, as these systems may perpetuate existing societal inequalities if not designed and monitored carefully.

Kurzweil's vision of the future includes not only the challenges posed by the Singularity but also its potential benefits. He argues that advancements in AI could lead to breakthroughs in medicine, such as personalized treatment plans and enhanced diagnostic capabilities. The integration of AI in healthcare could be expressed as:

$$H(t) = H_0 + B(t) \tag{14}$$

where $H(t)$ is the health outcomes at time t, H_0 is the baseline health outcomes, and $B(t)$ represents the benefits derived from AI integration.

In conclusion, exploring the concept of the Technological Singularity reveals a complex interplay of innovation, ethical considerations, and societal implications. As we stand on the precipice of a new era defined by rapid technological advancement, it is crucial to navigate these challenges with foresight and responsibility. The future may hold unimaginable possibilities, but it also demands a rigorous examination of the paths we choose to take.

Predictions and Prophecies

Raymond Kurzweil, a name synonymous with futurism and technological advancement, has made a plethora of predictions regarding the trajectory of artificial intelligence and its integration into human society. His foresight is not merely speculative; it is grounded in a profound understanding of exponential growth in technology, which he articulates through his law of accelerating returns. According to Kurzweil, technological progress is not linear but exponential, meaning that each advancement builds upon the previous ones at an increasing rate.

The Law of Accelerating Returns

Kurzweil's law can be mathematically expressed as follows:

$$T(n) = T(n-1) + k \cdot f(n) \tag{15}$$

where $T(n)$ is the time taken for a particular technological advancement at stage n, k is a constant representing the speed of progress, and $f(n)$ is a function that reflects the exponential nature of technological growth. This framework allows us to understand why Kurzweil believes that the next few decades will witness unprecedented advancements in AI and related fields.

Predictions for the 21st Century

One of Kurzweil's most notable predictions is that by the year 2029, machines will achieve human-level intelligence, a milestone often referred to as the point of "strong AI." This prediction is based on the historical trend of computational power doubling approximately every two years, a phenomenon encapsulated in

Moore's Law. Kurzweil argues that as we approach this threshold, the implications for society will be profound.

For instance, Kurzweil predicts that by the 2040s, we will witness the emergence of superintelligent AI, systems that surpass human cognitive abilities across virtually all domains. This superintelligence will not only enhance productivity but also drive innovations in medicine, education, and even creativity. He envisions a world where AI assists in solving complex problems such as climate change, disease eradication, and poverty alleviation.

The Role of AI in Society

Kurzweil's prophecies extend beyond mere technological capability; they delve into the societal implications of these advancements. He posits that as AI becomes more integrated into our daily lives, it will transform the workforce. While there are concerns regarding job displacement due to automation, Kurzweil argues that new industries will emerge, creating jobs that we cannot yet imagine. He famously stated, "The future will be about creating new jobs for people who will work alongside intelligent machines."

However, this optimistic view is not without its challenges. The transition to an AI-driven economy raises questions about the ethical implications of such technology. For instance, how do we ensure that AI systems are designed to align with human values? Kurzweil emphasizes the importance of ethical AI development, advocating for transparency and accountability in AI systems to mitigate risks associated with misuse.

Challenges and Potential Risks

Despite his optimistic outlook, Kurzweil acknowledges the potential risks of advanced AI. He warns of scenarios where AI could be weaponized or used to infringe on privacy rights. The rapid development of AI technologies can outpace regulatory frameworks, leading to a situation where society is unprepared for the consequences. For example, the rise of autonomous weapons systems raises ethical dilemmas regarding accountability in warfare.

Kurzweil also highlights the importance of addressing the digital divide, ensuring that the benefits of AI are accessible to all, rather than being concentrated in the hands of a few. He argues that education and policy must evolve in tandem with technology to prepare future generations for a world where AI plays a central role.

Conclusion

In summary, Kurzweil's predictions and prophecies regarding AI are both visionary and cautionary. They invite us to reflect on the trajectory of technological advancement and its implications for humanity. As we stand on the brink of a new era defined by intelligent machines, Kurzweil's insights serve as a roadmap for navigating the complexities of a future where humans and machines coexist, innovate, and redefine the very essence of existence.

The Impact of AI in the Future

The future impact of Artificial Intelligence (AI) is a topic of intense debate and speculation among technologists, ethicists, and the general public. As we stand on the precipice of a new technological era, it becomes imperative to understand the potential ramifications of AI on various facets of human life. This section delves into the various dimensions of AI's future impact, exploring opportunities, challenges, and theoretical frameworks that underpin this revolutionary technology.

Transformative Potential

AI is poised to transform industries, economies, and societies at large. According to a report by McKinsey Global Institute, it is estimated that AI could contribute an additional $13 trillion to the global economy by 2030, increasing global GDP by about 1.2% annually. This economic boon is expected to arise from increased productivity, automation of routine tasks, and the emergence of new markets driven by AI innovations.

Healthcare Revolution

One of the most promising applications of AI is in the healthcare sector. AI systems are being developed to assist in diagnostics, treatment recommendations, and patient management. For instance, IBM's Watson has demonstrated the ability to analyze vast amounts of medical literature and patient data to provide oncologists with evidence-based treatment options. This capability not only enhances the accuracy of diagnoses but also significantly reduces the time required for healthcare professionals to sift through data.

$$\text{AI Impact}_{health} = \frac{\text{Improved Outcomes} + \text{Cost Reduction}}{\text{Time Efficiency}} \tag{16}$$

This equation illustrates the multifaceted impact of AI in healthcare, where improved patient outcomes and cost reductions are weighed against the time efficiency gained through AI integration.

Economic Disruption and Job Market Transformation

While the economic benefits of AI are significant, the technology also poses challenges, particularly concerning the job market. The World Economic Forum predicts that by 2025, 85 million jobs may be displaced due to the shift in labor demand toward AI and automation. However, this displacement is expected to be offset by the creation of 97 million new roles that require distinctly human skills such as creativity, emotional intelligence, and problem-solving.

$$\text{Net Job Change} = \text{New Jobs Created} - \text{Jobs Displaced} \qquad (17)$$

This equation emphasizes the dynamic nature of the job market in the face of AI advancements. The challenge lies in ensuring that workers are equipped with the necessary skills to transition into new roles, necessitating a robust investment in education and training programs.

Ethical Considerations and Societal Impact

As AI systems become more integrated into society, ethical considerations will play a crucial role in shaping their development and deployment. Issues such as bias in AI algorithms, data privacy, and accountability for AI-driven decisions must be addressed to ensure that technology serves the public good. For example, facial recognition technology has raised concerns about racial bias and surveillance, prompting calls for regulation and oversight.

$$\text{Ethical Impact} = \frac{\text{Bias Reduction} + \text{Privacy Protection}}{\text{Accountability}} \qquad (18)$$

This equation illustrates the need for a balanced approach to AI ethics, where reducing bias and protecting privacy must be weighed against the accountability of AI systems.

AI in Education

The future of education is another arena where AI is expected to make significant strides. Personalized learning experiences powered by AI can adapt to individual student needs, enhancing engagement and improving learning outcomes. For instance, platforms like Coursera and Khan Academy utilize AI algorithms to recommend courses and resources tailored to students' learning styles and progress.

$$\text{Learning Efficiency} = \frac{\text{Personalization} \times \text{Engagement}}{\text{Time}} \qquad (19)$$

This formula signifies that the efficiency of learning can be maximized through personalization and engagement, which AI facilitates.

Conclusion

In conclusion, the impact of AI in the future is multifaceted, encompassing economic growth, healthcare advancements, job market transformations, ethical considerations, and educational enhancements. As we navigate this uncharted territory, it is essential to foster a collaborative dialogue among stakeholders, including technologists, policymakers, and the public, to harness the full potential of AI while mitigating its risks. The journey ahead is undoubtedly complex, but with thoughtful stewardship, AI can be a catalyst for positive change in society.

The Role of AI in Society

Artificial Intelligence (AI) has emerged as a transformative force in modern society, reshaping industries, redefining human interactions, and altering the very fabric of daily life. From healthcare to finance, education to entertainment, AI's influence is pervasive, promising both unprecedented advancements and complex challenges.

AI in Everyday Life

AI systems are now woven into the fabric of our everyday experiences. Virtual assistants like Siri, Alexa, and Google Assistant have become household names, helping users manage tasks, answer questions, and control smart home devices. According to a report by *Statista*, the global market for smart speakers alone is projected to reach $35 billion by 2025.

Transforming Industries

In the healthcare sector, AI technologies are revolutionizing diagnostics and treatment plans. Machine learning algorithms analyze medical data to predict patient outcomes, identify diseases at earlier stages, and personalize treatment options. For instance, IBM's Watson has demonstrated its capacity to analyze vast amounts of medical literature and patient data, assisting oncologists in making informed decisions. A study published in the *Journal of Oncology* found that Watson's recommendations matched expert oncologists' treatment decisions 93% of the time, underscoring AI's potential to enhance healthcare delivery.

In finance, AI-driven algorithms facilitate high-frequency trading, risk assessment, and fraud detection. Companies like JPMorgan Chase employ AI to analyze transaction patterns and detect anomalies, thereby reducing fraud losses. The use of AI in financial services is expected to save the industry $1 trillion by 2030, according to a report by *McKinsey*.

Education and AI

The educational landscape is also experiencing a paradigm shift due to AI. Personalized learning platforms, powered by adaptive learning technologies, tailor educational experiences to individual students' needs. For example, platforms like *Knewton* and *DreamBox Learning* utilize data analytics to adjust content in real-time, ensuring that students grasp concepts before progressing. This individualized approach can lead to improved educational outcomes, as evidenced by a study conducted by *The Bill and Melinda Gates Foundation*, which found that students using adaptive learning platforms performed better than their peers in traditional settings.

Ethical Considerations

Despite its potential, the integration of AI into society raises significant ethical concerns. Issues of bias, accountability, and transparency loom large. For instance, AI algorithms trained on historical data can perpetuate existing biases, leading to discriminatory outcomes. A notable example is the use of AI in hiring processes, where algorithms may favor candidates based on biased historical data, inadvertently disadvantaging qualified individuals from underrepresented groups.

$$\text{Bias}_{AI} = \frac{\text{Number of Discriminatory Outcomes}}{\text{Total Outcomes}} \tag{20}$$

This equation illustrates the importance of monitoring and mitigating bias in AI systems. Ensuring fairness in AI requires diverse training datasets, continuous evaluation, and the implementation of fairness-aware algorithms.

The Future of AI in Society

Looking ahead, the role of AI in society is poised to expand further, with implications for employment, privacy, and security. As AI automates routine tasks, concerns about job displacement arise. The *World Economic Forum* predicts that by 2025, 85 million jobs may be displaced due to AI, while 97 million new roles will emerge. This transition necessitates a robust approach to workforce reskilling and education to prepare individuals for the future job market.

Moreover, the proliferation of AI technologies raises questions about privacy and data security. With AI systems processing vast amounts of personal data, ensuring the protection of individual privacy is paramount. The implementation of regulations such as the General Data Protection Regulation (GDPR) in the European Union serves as a framework for addressing these concerns, emphasizing the need for transparency and user consent in data handling practices.

In conclusion, AI's role in society is multifaceted, encompassing both opportunities and challenges. As we navigate this evolving landscape, it is crucial to foster a dialogue around ethical considerations, promote inclusivity, and ensure that technological advancements benefit all segments of society. The future of AI hinges not only on technological innovation but also on our collective ability to address the ethical, social, and economic implications that accompany its integration into everyday life.

Challenges and Potential Risks

The advent of artificial intelligence (AI) heralds unprecedented opportunities for innovation and advancement; however, it also brings forth a myriad of challenges and potential risks that society must navigate. As we stand on the precipice of a future shaped by intelligent machines, it is crucial to examine these challenges in depth, considering both theoretical frameworks and real-world implications.

One of the primary challenges posed by AI is the issue of **autonomy**. As machines become increasingly capable of making decisions without human intervention, the question arises: who is responsible for the actions of these autonomous systems? This dilemma is particularly pronounced in sectors such as autonomous vehicles, where the consequences of a malfunction or decision made by an AI could result in catastrophic outcomes. The legal and ethical frameworks surrounding accountability must evolve to address these complexities.

$$\text{Autonomy} \rightarrow \text{Responsibility} \quad (\text{AI Decision-Making}) \quad (21)$$

Another significant risk associated with AI is **bias**. AI systems learn from data, and if that data is biased, the AI will perpetuate and even amplify these biases. For example, facial recognition technology has been shown to misidentify individuals of certain ethnic backgrounds at disproportionately higher rates. This not only raises ethical concerns but also poses risks to civil liberties and social justice. A notable study by Buolamwini and Gebru (2018) highlighted that commercial facial analysis algorithms exhibited higher error rates for darker-skinned individuals, particularly women, illustrating the potential for AI to reinforce existing societal inequities.

$$\text{Bias} \rightarrow \text{Discrimination} \quad (\text{AI Outcomes}) \tag{22}$$

The challenge of **job displacement** is another pressing concern. As AI systems become capable of performing tasks traditionally carried out by humans, there is a growing fear of widespread unemployment. According to a report by McKinsey Global Institute (2017), up to 800 million global workers could be displaced by automation by 2030. This transition could exacerbate economic inequality, as those with skills tailored to the demands of an AI-driven economy may thrive, while others may struggle to find new employment opportunities.

$$\text{Job Displacement} \rightarrow \text{Economic Inequality} \quad (\text{Labor Market}) \tag{23}$$

Moreover, the proliferation of AI raises concerns about **privacy**. As AI systems increasingly rely on vast amounts of personal data to function effectively, the potential for misuse of that data grows. High-profile data breaches and the unauthorized use of personal information have already demonstrated the vulnerabilities inherent in our digital landscape. The Cambridge Analytica scandal serves as a stark reminder of the dangers associated with data exploitation, prompting calls for stricter regulations and ethical standards in data management.

$$\text{Privacy} \rightarrow \text{Data Misuse} \quad (\text{Personal Information}) \tag{24}$$

The potential for **malicious use** of AI technologies is another critical risk. As AI becomes more accessible, there is the possibility that it could be weaponized or employed for nefarious purposes. For instance, AI-driven deepfake technology has already been used to create convincing but false media content, leading to misinformation and manipulation. The implications of such technologies on public trust and democratic processes cannot be overstated.

$$\text{Malicious Use} \rightarrow \text{Misinformation} \quad (\text{Deepfakes}) \tag{25}$$

Lastly, the concept of **existential risk** cannot be overlooked. As theorized by Nick Bostrom (2014), the development of superintelligent AI could pose a threat to humanity itself if not aligned with human values. The fear is that an AI with goals misaligned with our own could pursue those goals in ways that are detrimental to human existence. This underscores the importance of incorporating robust safety measures and ethical considerations into the development of AI systems.

$$\text{Superintelligence} \rightarrow \text{Existential Risk} \quad (\text{Human Survival}) \quad (26)$$

In conclusion, while the potential benefits of AI are vast, the challenges and risks associated with its integration into society are equally significant. As we navigate this uncharted territory, it is imperative that we engage in thoughtful discourse, establish comprehensive regulatory frameworks, and prioritize ethical considerations to ensure that the evolution of AI serves humanity positively rather than jeopardizing it. The future of AI is not just a technological challenge; it is a profound moral and philosophical undertaking that will shape the very fabric of our society.

Criticisms and Controversies

Raymond Kurzweil, often heralded as a visionary in the fields of artificial intelligence and futurism, has not been without his share of criticisms and controversies. His bold predictions regarding the future of technology, particularly in relation to the concept of the Singularity, have sparked intense debate among scholars, technologists, and ethicists alike. This section explores some of the key criticisms leveled against Kurzweil's ideas and the controversies that have arisen from his work.

Skepticism Towards Predictions

One of the most prominent criticisms of Kurzweil's work stems from his optimistic forecasts about technological advancement. Kurzweil's predictions often suggest exponential growth in technology, particularly in artificial intelligence, leading to a point where machines surpass human intelligence, commonly referred to as the Singularity. Critics argue that such predictions are overly optimistic and lack empirical support.

For example, Kurzweil famously predicted that by 2029, machines would be able to pass the Turing Test, demonstrating human-like intelligence. However, many AI researchers contend that the complexities of human cognition and emotional intelligence cannot be reduced to mere computational power. The Turing Test itself has been criticized for being an inadequate measure of true intelligence, as it focuses solely on conversational ability rather than understanding or consciousness.

Technological Determinism

Another area of contention is Kurzweil's perceived embrace of technological determinism—the idea that technology develops according to its own logic, independent of social factors. Critics argue that this perspective overlooks the socio-political context in which technology is developed and deployed. For instance, the rapid advancement of AI technologies raises questions about who controls these technologies and for what purposes.

Kurzweil's vision of a future where AI enhances human capabilities and leads to a utopian society does not account for potential misuse of technology, such as surveillance, manipulation, and the exacerbation of social inequalities. This has led to concerns that Kurzweil's framework may inadvertently support a laissez-faire approach to technology regulation, potentially allowing harmful practices to proliferate unchecked.

Ethical Implications

The ethical implications of Kurzweil's work have also been a source of controversy. His advocacy for human enhancement through technology, including brain-computer interfaces and genetic modifications, raises profound ethical questions about what it means to be human. Critics argue that such enhancements could lead to a societal divide between those who can afford these technologies and those who cannot, creating a new class of "enhanced" individuals.

Kurzweil's assertion that merging with machines will lead to a form of immortality has been met with skepticism. While the prospect of extending human life is enticing, the ethical considerations surrounding consent, identity, and the definition of life itself are complex and fraught with moral dilemmas. For instance, if an individual's consciousness were to be uploaded to a machine, would that entity still be considered the same person? Such questions challenge our understanding of identity and existence.

Critique from the AI Community

Within the AI community, Kurzweil's ideas have also faced scrutiny. Some researchers argue that his focus on singularity and superintelligence detracts from pressing issues in the field, such as bias in AI algorithms, accountability, and transparency. The emphasis on achieving human-like intelligence can overshadow critical discussions about the ethical deployment of AI technologies in real-world applications.

Moreover, Kurzweil's approach to AI development has been criticized for being overly simplistic. The notion that intelligence can be distilled into algorithms and computations fails to account for the nuances of human cognition, emotion, and social interaction. This reductionist view may lead to the development of AI systems that lack the depth and breadth of human understanding, potentially resulting in unintended consequences.

Public Perception and Media Representation

Lastly, Kurzweil's public persona and the media's portrayal of his work have contributed to controversies surrounding his ideas. His charismatic speaking style and ability to articulate complex concepts in an accessible manner have garnered a substantial following. However, this has also led to a phenomenon known as "techno-optimism," where the public may uncritically accept his predictions without engaging with the underlying complexities and potential risks.

The media often highlights Kurzweil's more sensational claims, such as the promise of immortality through technology, which can lead to misconceptions about the feasibility and ethical implications of such advancements. This oversimplification can foster a culture of uncritical acceptance of technological solutions to deeply rooted societal problems.

Conclusion

In conclusion, while Raymond Kurzweil's contributions to the fields of AI and futurism are undeniable, the criticisms and controversies surrounding his work highlight the need for a nuanced understanding of technology's role in society. As we navigate the complexities of AI and its implications for the future, it is essential to engage with these critiques to ensure that technological advancements serve the greater good and do not exacerbate existing inequalities or ethical dilemmas. The dialogue between optimism and skepticism is crucial as we move toward an increasingly technologically integrated world.

Ethical Considerations of AI

The rapid advancement of artificial intelligence (AI) technologies has brought forth a myriad of ethical considerations that demand our attention. As we stand on the precipice of a new era marked by unprecedented capabilities in machine learning, natural language processing, and autonomous systems, it is imperative to navigate the ethical landscape with caution and foresight.

The Moral Framework of AI

At the core of ethical considerations in AI lies the question of moral agency. Can machines be held accountable for their actions? Traditional ethical theories, such as utilitarianism, deontology, and virtue ethics, provide frameworks for evaluating the implications of AI decisions. For instance, utilitarianism, which advocates for actions that maximize overall happiness, prompts us to consider whether AI systems contribute positively to societal well-being.

$$\text{Utility} = \sum_{i=1}^{n} \text{Happiness}_i - \text{Suffering}_i \qquad (27)$$

In contrast, deontological ethics emphasizes duty and adherence to rules. This perspective raises concerns about the potential for AI to make decisions that violate established ethical norms, such as privacy and fairness.

Bias and Fairness

One of the most pressing ethical issues in AI is the presence of bias in algorithms. AI systems learn from data, and if the data reflects societal biases, the AI will perpetuate and even exacerbate these biases. For example, facial recognition technologies have been shown to have higher error rates for individuals with darker skin tones, leading to disproportionate misidentification and wrongful accusations.

To illustrate this point, consider the following equation representing the fairness of an AI system:

$$\text{Fairness} = \frac{\text{True Positives} + \text{True Negatives}}{\text{Total Population}} \qquad (28)$$

If the true positives and negatives are skewed due to biased training data, the fairness metric diminishes, highlighting the need for rigorous data auditing and algorithmic transparency.

Privacy Concerns

The integration of AI into everyday life raises significant privacy concerns. AI systems often require vast amounts of personal data to function effectively, leading to potential infringements on individual privacy rights. The ethical principle of respect for autonomy demands that individuals have control over their personal information.

Consider the implications of AI-driven surveillance systems that monitor public spaces. While such technologies can enhance security, they also pose a threat to civil liberties. The equation representing the trade-off between security and privacy can be expressed as follows:

$$\text{Net Benefit} = \text{Security Benefits} - \text{Privacy Costs} \qquad (29)$$

Balancing these competing interests is a critical ethical challenge for policymakers and technologists alike.

Job Displacement and Economic Inequality

The rise of AI also brings forth concerns about job displacement and economic inequality. As machines become increasingly capable of performing tasks traditionally done by humans, there is a legitimate fear that widespread unemployment may ensue. This could exacerbate existing inequalities, as those with lower skill levels may find it increasingly difficult to secure stable employment.

The ethical implications of such economic disruption require careful consideration. The following equation can be used to assess the impact of AI on employment:

$$\text{Employment Impact} = \text{Job Creation} - \text{Job Displacement} \qquad (30)$$

If job displacement outpaces job creation, we must address the ethical responsibility of those developing AI technologies to consider the societal ramifications of their innovations.

The Role of Regulation

Given the profound ethical implications of AI, the role of regulation becomes paramount. Policymakers must establish guidelines that ensure the responsible development and deployment of AI technologies. This includes creating standards for transparency, accountability, and fairness in AI systems.

For instance, the European Union's General Data Protection Regulation (GDPR) includes provisions that address data protection and privacy, setting a precedent for ethical AI governance. The equation for regulatory effectiveness can be framed as:

$$\text{Regulatory Effectiveness} = \frac{\text{Compliance Rate}}{\text{Total AI Systems}} \qquad (31)$$

A high compliance rate indicates a successful regulatory framework that upholds ethical standards in AI.

Conclusion

In conclusion, the ethical considerations surrounding AI are complex and multifaceted. As we continue to innovate and integrate AI into various aspects of our lives, it is essential to maintain a dialogue about the ethical implications of our technological choices. By grounding our discussions in established ethical frameworks and fostering collaboration among technologists, ethicists, and policymakers, we can strive to ensure that AI serves humanity in a manner that is just, fair, and responsible. The future of AI is not solely a technological challenge; it is fundamentally an ethical one that requires our collective vigilance and commitment.

Privacy Concerns with AI

As artificial intelligence (AI) continues to evolve and integrate into our daily lives, the issue of privacy has emerged as a significant concern. With the ability to process vast amounts of data, AI systems can inadvertently or deliberately infringe upon individual privacy rights. This section explores the theoretical underpinnings of privacy in the context of AI, the problems that arise, and pertinent examples that illustrate these challenges.

Theoretical Framework of Privacy

Privacy, in the context of technology, can be understood through several theoretical lenses. One foundational theory is the concept of *informational privacy*, which posits that individuals have the right to control their personal information and determine how it is collected, used, and shared. Westin (1967) defines privacy as "the claim of individuals, groups, or institutions to determine for themselves when, how, and to what extent information about them is communicated to others."

In the realm of AI, this theory is challenged by the very nature of data collection and processing. AI systems often rely on *big data*, which aggregates information from various sources, including social media, online transactions, and even IoT devices. This aggregation can lead to a loss of control over personal data, as individuals may not be aware of what information is being collected or how it is being used.

Problems Arising from AI and Privacy

The intersection of AI and privacy raises several critical problems:

- **Data Collection and Surveillance:** AI systems often require extensive data to function effectively, leading to pervasive surveillance. For instance, facial recognition technology has been deployed in public spaces, raising concerns about constant monitoring and the potential for misuse by authorities.

- **Informed Consent:** Many users unknowingly consent to data collection through lengthy terms of service agreements. The complexity of these documents often obscures the extent to which personal information will be utilized, undermining the principle of informed consent.

- **Data Breaches:** The centralization of data in AI systems makes them attractive targets for cyberattacks. High-profile data breaches, such as the Equifax incident in 2017, expose millions of individuals' personal information, leading to identity theft and financial fraud.

- **Algorithmic Bias:** AI systems can perpetuate existing biases in data, leading to discriminatory outcomes. For example, biased algorithms in hiring processes may unfairly disadvantage candidates based on race or gender, raising ethical concerns about fairness and transparency.

Examples of Privacy Concerns in AI

Several real-world examples highlight the privacy concerns associated with AI:

- **Cambridge Analytica Scandal:** In 2018, it was revealed that the political consulting firm Cambridge Analytica harvested personal data from millions of Facebook users without their consent. This data was used to create targeted political advertisements, raising alarms about the misuse of personal information and the lack of regulatory oversight in data practices.

- **Facial Recognition Technology:** Cities like San Francisco and Boston have enacted bans on facial recognition technology due to concerns about privacy violations and racial profiling. Studies have shown that these systems can misidentify individuals, leading to wrongful accusations and a chilling effect on public behavior.

+ **Smart Home Devices:** Devices such as Amazon's Alexa and Google Home collect voice data to enhance user experience. However, there have been instances where these devices inadvertently record private conversations, raising concerns about data retention and unauthorized access to sensitive information.

Regulatory and Ethical Considerations

Addressing privacy concerns in AI necessitates a multi-faceted approach that includes regulatory frameworks and ethical considerations. The General Data Protection Regulation (GDPR) in the European Union serves as a model for protecting personal data, emphasizing transparency, consent, and the right to be forgotten. However, enforcement remains a challenge, particularly with the global nature of technology companies.

Ethically, developers and organizations must prioritize privacy by design, ensuring that AI systems are built with privacy considerations from the outset. This includes implementing robust data anonymization techniques, conducting regular privacy impact assessments, and fostering a culture of accountability.

Conclusion

The privacy concerns associated with AI are complex and multifaceted, encompassing theoretical, practical, and ethical dimensions. As AI continues to permeate various aspects of life, it is imperative to address these concerns proactively. By prioritizing privacy, fostering transparency, and adhering to ethical standards, society can harness the benefits of AI while safeguarding individual rights. The future of AI must not only be innovative but also respectful of the privacy that underpins human dignity and autonomy.

AI and the Job Market

The advent of artificial intelligence (AI) has brought forth a transformative wave across various industries, leading to significant changes in the job market. As AI systems become increasingly sophisticated, they are capable of performing tasks that were once thought to be the exclusive domain of human workers. This section explores the implications of AI on employment, the challenges it poses, and the opportunities it creates.

The Automation of Jobs

One of the most immediate effects of AI on the job market is the automation of routine and repetitive tasks. Industries such as manufacturing, logistics, and customer service have seen a substantial increase in the deployment of AI-driven systems that can perform tasks with speed and accuracy. For instance, in manufacturing, robots equipped with AI algorithms can assemble products, monitor quality, and even manage supply chains.

The impact of automation can be illustrated through the following equation:

$$\text{Job Loss} = \text{Jobs Automated} - \text{New Jobs Created} \qquad (32)$$

This equation highlights the balance between jobs lost due to automation and those created through new technologies. While many low-skilled jobs are at risk, it is essential to recognize that AI also has the potential to create new job opportunities in sectors that require advanced skills.

Shifting Skill Requirements

As AI systems take over routine tasks, the demand for higher-level skills is increasing. Workers are now expected to possess competencies that enable them to work alongside AI technologies, such as data analysis, programming, and critical thinking. This shift necessitates a reevaluation of educational and training programs to equip the workforce with the necessary skills for the future job market.

For example, a report by the World Economic Forum (2020) predicts that by 2025, 85 million jobs may be displaced by a shift in labor between humans and machines. However, it also forecasts that 97 million new roles may emerge that are more adapted to the new division of labor between humans, machines, and algorithms. This emphasizes the importance of upskilling and reskilling initiatives to prepare the workforce for these changes.

Job Displacement vs. Job Creation

The debate surrounding AI and the job market often centers on the fear of job displacement. While it is true that some jobs will become obsolete, history has shown that technological advancements often lead to the creation of new job categories. For instance, the rise of the internet led to the emergence of roles such as web developers, digital marketers, and data scientists—positions that did not exist before.

A study by McKinsey & Company (2017) found that while 61% of jobs are susceptible to automation, only a fraction will be entirely eliminated. Many roles will evolve, requiring workers to adapt to new tools and processes. For example, in healthcare, AI can assist doctors in diagnosing diseases, but it cannot replace the human touch and empathy required in patient care.

The Gig Economy and Flexible Work

AI is also contributing to the growth of the gig economy, where individuals take on short-term contracts or freelance work rather than traditional full-time employment. Platforms powered by AI, such as Uber and TaskRabbit, connect workers with opportunities based on demand. This flexibility allows workers to choose when and how much they work, but it also raises concerns about job security and benefits.

The gig economy exemplifies the changing nature of work in the age of AI. As traditional employment models evolve, workers may need to embrace a more entrepreneurial mindset, seeking out multiple income streams and adapting to a rapidly changing job landscape.

Addressing the Challenges

While AI presents numerous opportunities, it also poses significant challenges that need to be addressed. Policymakers, educators, and business leaders must collaborate to create frameworks that support workers during this transition. This includes:

- **Investment in Education and Training:** Governments and organizations should invest in education and training programs that focus on skills relevant to the AI-driven economy.

- **Support for Displaced Workers:** Implementing safety nets and retraining programs for workers displaced by automation is crucial to ensure a smooth transition.

- **Encouraging Innovation:** Fostering a culture of innovation can lead to the development of new industries and job opportunities that leverage AI technologies.

Conclusion

In conclusion, the relationship between AI and the job market is complex and multifaceted. While AI has the potential to displace certain jobs, it also offers opportunities for job creation and the evolution of the workforce. By embracing change and investing in education and training, society can harness the power of AI to create a more dynamic and inclusive job market. The future of work will undoubtedly be shaped by technological advancements, and it is essential to navigate this landscape thoughtfully and proactively.

The Art of Transcendence

Merging Man and Machine

The concept of merging man and machine has long been a subject of fascination for scientists, philosophers, and futurists alike. At the heart of this exploration lies the potential to enhance human capabilities through technology, creating a new paradigm where the lines between biological and artificial intelligence blur. This section delves into the theoretical frameworks, challenges, and real-world examples of this profound integration.

Theoretical Frameworks

The merging of man and machine can be understood through several theoretical lenses, including cybernetics, transhumanism, and the philosophy of mind.

Cybernetics is a field that studies the control and communication in animals and machines. Norbert Wiener, the father of cybernetics, posited that both biological and mechanical systems can be analyzed through feedback loops. The equation governing feedback systems can be expressed as:

$$Y(t) = G \cdot X(t) + H \cdot Y(t-1) \tag{33}$$

where $Y(t)$ is the output at time t, $X(t)$ is the input, G is the gain of the system, and H is the feedback coefficient. This equation illustrates how both human cognition and machine responses can be modeled similarly, emphasizing the potential for integration.

Transhumanism advocates for the use of technology to enhance the human condition. Proponents argue that through genetic engineering, nanotechnology, and cognitive enhancement, humans can transcend their biological limitations. The transhumanist manifesto, penned by thinkers like Max More, outlines a vision for a post-human future where individuals can choose to augment their physical and mental capabilities.

Philosophy of Mind raises critical questions about consciousness and identity. Theories such as functionalism suggest that mental states are defined by their functional roles rather than their physical substrates. This perspective opens the door to the possibility that machines could possess forms of consciousness, challenging our understanding of what it means to be human.

Challenges in Merging Man and Machine

While the potential for merging man and machine is enticing, several challenges must be addressed:

Ethical Considerations arise when discussing the implications of cognitive enhancement and identity. If individuals can enhance their intelligence or physical abilities through technology, what does this mean for equality and access? The risk of creating a socio-economic divide between enhanced and non-enhanced individuals is a pressing concern.

Technological Limitations also pose significant hurdles. Current brain-computer interfaces (BCIs) have made strides in allowing communication between the brain and external devices. However, the technology is still in its infancy. For instance, while companies like Neuralink are developing devices that can read brain signals, the complexity of human cognition presents a formidable challenge. The relationship between neurons and their electrical signals can be modeled using the Hodgkin-Huxley equations, which describe the action potentials in neurons:

$$C_m \frac{dV}{dt} = I_{ion} + I_{ext} \tag{34}$$

where C_m is the membrane capacitance, V is the membrane potential, I_{ion} is the ionic current, and I_{ext} is the external current. The intricacies of these interactions complicate the development of effective BCIs that can seamlessly integrate with the human brain.

Psychological Impacts of merging human cognition with machines must also be considered. The fear of losing one's identity or autonomy in the face of increasing technological integration is a legitimate concern. As humans become more reliant on technology for cognitive tasks, questions arise about the preservation of individual agency and the essence of human experience.

Real-World Examples

Despite the challenges, several real-world examples illustrate the potential of merging man and machine:

Brain-Computer Interfaces (BCIs) have shown promise in assisting individuals with disabilities. For instance, the work of the BrainGate consortium has demonstrated that paralyzed individuals can control robotic limbs using their thoughts alone. This groundbreaking research utilizes implanted electrodes to detect neural activity, translating it into movement commands for external devices.

Cognitive Enhancement Technologies are also emerging. Companies like Kernel are developing non-invasive devices aimed at enhancing cognitive function through neurostimulation. Early studies suggest that such technologies may improve memory and attention, paving the way for a future where cognitive enhancement becomes commonplace.

Virtual Reality (VR) and Augmented Reality (AR) technologies are further examples of merging man and machine. By creating immersive environments that can interact with users' sensory perceptions, VR and AR have the potential to enhance learning, training, and even therapeutic practices. For instance, VR has been successfully used in exposure therapy for PTSD, allowing patients to confront their fears in a controlled and safe environment.

Conclusion

The merging of man and machine presents a complex tapestry of opportunities and challenges. As we stand on the brink of a new era defined by technological integration, it is imperative to navigate the ethical, psychological, and technological landscapes thoughtfully. The journey towards a future where humans and machines coexist and enhance one another is not merely a technical endeavor; it is a profound exploration of what it means to be human in an increasingly digital world. As Raymond Kurzweil himself posits, the future may not just be about machines augmenting human capabilities, but rather about redefining the very essence of humanity itself.

Advancements in Brain-Computer Interface

The concept of Brain-Computer Interfaces (BCIs) has evolved significantly since its inception, driven by the desire to bridge the gap between human cognition and machine intelligence. BCIs allow for direct communication between the brain and external devices, enabling a myriad of applications ranging from medical rehabilitation to enhanced human capabilities. This section delves into the advancements in BCIs, exploring their theoretical foundations, practical challenges, and groundbreaking examples that highlight their transformative potential.

Theoretical Foundations

At the heart of BCIs lies the principle of neuroplasticity, which refers to the brain's ability to reorganize itself by forming new neural connections throughout life. This adaptability is crucial for the successful implementation of BCIs, as it allows users to learn how to control devices through thought alone. The primary goal of BCIs is to decode brain signals, which can be modeled mathematically.

The relationship between neural activity and the resultant signals can be expressed through the following equation:

$$S(t) = \sum_{i=1}^{N} w_i \cdot A_i(t) \tag{35}$$

where $S(t)$ represents the signal at time t, w_i are the weights assigned to each neural signal, and $A_i(t)$ represents the activity of the i-th neuron at time t.

The challenge lies in accurately interpreting these signals, which can be influenced by various factors, including noise and signal degradation. Advanced signal processing techniques, such as machine learning algorithms, are increasingly employed to enhance the accuracy of BCI systems.

Challenges in BCI Development

Despite the promising advancements, several challenges remain in the development and implementation of BCIs.

- **Signal Quality:** The quality of signals obtained from the brain is often compromised due to external noise and biological variability. Techniques such as filtering and artifact removal are essential to improve signal integrity.

- **User Variability:** Each individual's neural patterns are unique, which complicates the generalization of BCI systems. Customization and adaptive learning algorithms are necessary to tailor BCIs to individual users.

- **Ethical Considerations:** The invasive nature of some BCI technologies raises ethical concerns regarding privacy, consent, and potential misuse. These issues must be carefully addressed to ensure responsible development.

Groundbreaking Examples

Several groundbreaking examples of BCI technology demonstrate its transformative potential across various fields:

- **Neuroprosthetics:** One of the most notable applications of BCIs is in neuroprosthetics, where devices restore function to individuals with motor impairments. For instance, the BrainGate system allows paralyzed individuals to control robotic arms using their thoughts, showcasing the profound impact of BCIs on rehabilitation and independence.

- **Cognitive Enhancement:** BCIs are also being explored for cognitive enhancement. Companies like Kernel are developing non-invasive BCIs aimed at improving memory and cognitive functions. These devices leverage brain stimulation techniques to enhance neural activity, potentially leading to improved learning capabilities.

- **Communication Aids:** BCIs have revolutionized communication for individuals with severe disabilities. The use of electroencephalography (EEG) to control communication devices enables users to convey thoughts and emotions without physical movement. This is exemplified by systems like the P300 speller, which allows users to select letters on a screen through focused attention.

Future Directions

As research in BCIs continues to advance, several promising directions are emerging:

- **Integration with AI:** The integration of artificial intelligence with BCIs holds the potential to create more intuitive and responsive systems. Machine learning algorithms can enhance the decoding of brain signals, allowing for more seamless interaction between humans and machines.

- **Non-Invasive Techniques:** Ongoing research into non-invasive BCI technologies aims to make these systems more accessible. Innovations such as functional near-infrared spectroscopy (fNIRS) and advanced EEG techniques are paving the way for safer and more user-friendly interfaces.

- **Ethical Frameworks:** As BCIs become more prevalent, the establishment of ethical frameworks is essential to address concerns related to privacy, consent, and the potential for cognitive manipulation. Stakeholders must collaborate to create guidelines that ensure the responsible use of BCI technology.

In conclusion, advancements in Brain-Computer Interfaces represent a remarkable intersection of neuroscience and technology, offering transformative possibilities for communication, rehabilitation, and cognitive enhancement. As we continue to explore the frontiers of this field, it is imperative to navigate the challenges and ethical considerations that accompany such groundbreaking innovations. The future of BCIs holds the promise of not only enhancing human capabilities but also redefining the very nature of our interaction with technology.

Ethical and Philosophical Implications

The interplay between artificial intelligence (AI) and human existence raises a plethora of ethical and philosophical questions that challenge our understanding of identity, morality, and the very fabric of society. As Raymond Kurzweil posits, the merging of man and machine is not merely a technological endeavor; it is a profound transformation that compels us to reconsider our values and responsibilities.

The Nature of Consciousness

One of the most pressing philosophical implications of advancing AI technologies is the question of consciousness. If we develop machines that can mimic human thought processes, at what point do we attribute consciousness to these entities? The Turing Test, proposed by Alan Turing, serves as a foundational concept in this discussion. Turing suggested that if a machine could engage in a conversation indistinguishable from that of a human, it could be considered intelligent. However, this raises further questions: Is intelligence synonymous with consciousness? Can a machine possess subjective experiences, or is it merely simulating responses based on algorithms?

$$C = f(I, E) \tag{36}$$

Where C represents consciousness, I represents intelligence, and E represents experience. This equation suggests that consciousness may depend on both intelligence and the capacity for experience. The implications of this relationship

THE ART OF TRANSCENDENCE   47

are profound, as they challenge our traditional views of what it means to be alive and sentient.

Moral Agency and Responsibility

As AI systems become more autonomous, the question of moral agency emerges. If an AI system makes a decision that leads to harm, who is responsible? Is it the programmer, the user, or the machine itself? This dilemma is particularly relevant in autonomous vehicles, where decisions made by AI can have life-or-death consequences. The concept of the "moral machine" explores how AI should be programmed to make ethical decisions. For instance, should an autonomous vehicle prioritize the safety of its passengers over pedestrians in a potential accident scenario?

$$R = \frac{H}{C} \qquad (37)$$

Where R is responsibility, H is harm caused, and C is the capacity for moral reasoning. This equation implies that as the capacity for moral reasoning in AI increases, so does the potential for responsibility in the event of harm.

Privacy and Surveillance

The integration of AI into everyday life also raises significant privacy concerns. With the ability to process vast amounts of data, AI systems can track individual behaviors, preferences, and even predict future actions. This capability can lead to a surveillance state where personal freedoms are compromised in the name of security and efficiency. The ethical implications of such surveillance are profound; they challenge our notions of autonomy and consent.

Consider the case of facial recognition technology, which has been implemented in various public spaces. While proponents argue that it enhances security, critics raise concerns about its potential for misuse and the erosion of privacy. The ethical question becomes: To what extent are we willing to sacrifice privacy for perceived safety?

The Digital Divide and Inequality

As AI technologies advance, they also risk exacerbating existing inequalities. The digital divide—the gap between those who have access to technology and those who do not—poses a significant ethical challenge. If only a privileged few can leverage AI for personal and professional gain, the gap between the haves and have-nots will widen, leading to societal discord. Kurzweil's vision of a future where AI enhances human capabilities must also consider how to ensure equitable access to these advancements.

$$D = \frac{A}{R} \tag{38}$$

Where D represents the digital divide, A represents access to technology, and R represents resources. As access to technology becomes more limited, the digital divide will grow, posing ethical questions about fairness and justice in a rapidly evolving technological landscape.

The Future of Human Identity

Finally, the merging of human and machine raises existential questions about the future of human identity. As we enhance our cognitive abilities through technology, what does it mean to be human? The philosophical implications of identity and selfhood become increasingly complex as we integrate AI into our lives. Kurzweil's notion of the "Singularity"—a point at which technological growth becomes uncontrollable and irreversible—forces us to confront the potential for a post-human future where traditional concepts of identity may no longer apply.

In conclusion, the ethical and philosophical implications of AI are vast and multifaceted. As we navigate this uncharted territory, it is imperative that we engage in thoughtful discourse about our values and responsibilities. The future of AI will not only shape our technological landscape but also redefine what it means to be human in an increasingly complex world.

The Impact of AI on Human Identity

As we stand on the precipice of a new technological era, the integration of artificial intelligence (AI) into our daily lives prompts profound questions about the nature of human identity. The advent of AI challenges traditional notions of what it means to be human, raising philosophical and ethical dilemmas that have captivated thinkers across disciplines. This section explores the multifaceted impact of AI on human identity, examining how our understanding of self is evolving in an increasingly digital world.

Redefining Human Experience

AI's ability to mimic human cognition and behavior blurs the lines between human and machine. As AI systems become more sophisticated, the distinction between human thought and machine processing becomes less clear. For instance, consider the development of natural language processing models like OpenAI's GPT-3, which can generate text that closely resembles human writing. This raises the question: if a machine can produce human-like responses, what does it mean to be human?

The philosopher John Searle's Chinese Room argument posits that understanding is not merely about processing information but involves conscious awareness and intentionality. While AI can simulate conversation, it lacks true understanding and consciousness. This distinction is crucial as we grapple with the implications of AI on our identity. If we begin to attribute human-like qualities to machines, we risk redefining our own humanity in relation to these entities.

The Role of AI in Self-Perception

AI also influences how individuals perceive themselves. Social media platforms, powered by AI algorithms, curate content that shapes our identities and self-image. The feedback loop created by likes, shares, and comments can lead to an altered self-perception. For example, a study by the Pew Research Center found that 69% of teens believe social media has a positive impact on their ability to connect with others, yet 60% also feel pressure to post content that will garner likes and approval.

This phenomenon can lead to a fragmented identity, where individuals present curated versions of themselves online, often at the expense of authenticity. The philosopher Sherry Turkle argues that technology can create a sense of connection while simultaneously fostering isolation. As we navigate our digital identities, we must confront the question of whether our online personas reflect our true selves or if they are mere facades constructed to meet societal expectations.

AI and the Evolution of Consciousness

The potential for AI to enhance human cognitive abilities raises further questions about identity. Technologies such as brain-computer interfaces (BCIs) aim to augment human cognition, allowing for direct communication between the brain and external devices. While these advancements hold promise for treating neurological disorders, they also challenge the notion of a singular, unaltered self.

Consider the work of Elon Musk's Neuralink, which seeks to create a symbiotic relationship between humans and machines. As individuals integrate AI into their cognitive processes, the line between human thought and machine assistance may blur. This evolution of consciousness prompts us to reconsider what it means to be human in a world where our minds can be augmented by technology.

Ethical Considerations and Identity

The integration of AI into our lives also raises ethical concerns regarding identity. As AI systems become more autonomous, questions arise about accountability and agency. For instance, if an AI system makes a decision that leads to harm, who is responsible? The developer, the user, or the machine itself? This dilemma complicates our understanding of identity, as we must consider the implications of agency in a world where machines can act independently.

Moreover, the potential for AI to manipulate human behavior poses risks to individual autonomy. Algorithms designed to maximize engagement can exploit psychological vulnerabilities, influencing our choices in ways we may not fully understand. This manipulation challenges our concept of free will, as our decisions may be shaped by unseen forces within AI systems.

Conclusion: Navigating the New Identity Landscape

In conclusion, the impact of AI on human identity is a complex and evolving discourse that necessitates careful consideration. As we embrace the opportunities presented by AI, we must also confront the challenges it poses to our understanding of self. The interplay between human and machine raises fundamental questions about consciousness, authenticity, and agency that will shape our identities in the years to come.

As we navigate this new identity landscape, it is imperative that we engage in ongoing dialogue about the ethical implications of AI. By fostering a critical understanding of our relationship with technology, we can strive to ensure that our identities remain rooted in our humanity, even as we venture into an increasingly AI-driven future.

Moral Considerations of Enhancing Human Intelligence

The pursuit of enhancing human intelligence through technology raises profound moral considerations that challenge our understanding of identity, autonomy, and the essence of being human. As we stand on the brink of a new era defined by artificial intelligence and cognitive enhancement, it is essential to navigate the ethical landscape that accompanies these advancements.

The Nature of Intelligence Enhancement

At its core, intelligence enhancement can be understood as the application of technology to improve cognitive abilities, memory, learning capacity, and problem-solving skills. This can take various forms, including pharmacological interventions, genetic modifications, and brain-computer interfaces (BCIs). Each method presents unique ethical dilemmas.

For instance, pharmacological enhancements, such as nootropics, aim to boost cognitive function. While they may offer benefits, they also raise questions about fairness and accessibility. If only a select few can afford these enhancements, we risk creating a cognitive divide, exacerbating existing social inequalities.

Autonomy and Consent

A critical moral consideration involves the autonomy of individuals in choosing to enhance their intelligence. The concept of informed consent is paramount. Individuals must be fully aware of the risks, benefits, and long-term implications of cognitive enhancements. The challenge lies in ensuring that consent is genuinely informed, particularly when dealing with vulnerable populations who may feel pressured to enhance their abilities to compete in a demanding society.

Furthermore, the potential for coercion looms large. In a world where cognitive enhancement becomes the norm, individuals may feel compelled to enhance their intelligence to keep up with peers or meet societal expectations. This raises the question of whether true autonomy can exist in such a context.

Identity and the Human Experience

Enhancing intelligence also prompts us to reflect on the very nature of human identity. What does it mean to be human in a world where cognitive abilities can be artificially augmented? Philosophers like Nick Bostrom and Eliezer Yudkowsky have explored these questions in depth, arguing that enhancing intelligence could lead to a divergence in human experience.

If we redefine intelligence through technological means, we must consider the implications for personal identity. Are enhanced individuals still fundamentally human, or do they represent a new class of beings? This question challenges our understanding of what it means to possess consciousness, creativity, and emotional depth.

The Risk of Dehumanization

One of the most pressing moral concerns is the potential for dehumanization. As we increasingly rely on technology to enhance our cognitive capacities, there is a risk of reducing individuals to mere algorithms or data points. This reductionist view can strip away the richness of human experience, creativity, and emotional intelligence, which are difficult to quantify or replicate through technology.

Moreover, the pursuit of enhanced intelligence may lead to a utilitarian approach to human life, where individuals are valued solely for their cognitive output. This perspective can foster a culture that prioritizes efficiency and productivity over empathy, compassion, and the intrinsic worth of every individual.

The Ethical Implications of AI and Cognitive Enhancement

The intersection of artificial intelligence and cognitive enhancement introduces additional ethical complexities. As AI systems become more capable, the question arises: should we enhance human intelligence to keep pace with machines? This concern is articulated in the concept of the "intelligence explosion," where the rapid advancement of AI could outstrip human cognitive abilities, leading to a scenario where humans are rendered obsolete.

This raises moral questions about our responsibility to ensure that technological advancements benefit humanity as a whole rather than exacerbate existing inequalities. The potential for AI to surpass human intelligence also necessitates a reevaluation of our ethical frameworks. How do we ensure that AI systems align with human values and do not undermine our moral agency?

Examples of Cognitive Enhancement in Practice

Several real-world examples illustrate the moral considerations surrounding cognitive enhancement. For instance, the use of Ritalin and Adderall among students for academic performance has sparked debates about fairness and the pressure to perform. While these medications can aid those with attention disorders, their misuse by healthy individuals raises ethical questions about the normalization of enhancement.

Similarly, advancements in BCIs, such as Elon Musk's Neuralink, promise to bridge the gap between human cognition and machines. While the potential benefits are vast, including improved memory and learning capabilities, the moral implications of merging human consciousness with technology are profound. We must consider who has access to such enhancements and the societal impact of creating a class of "superhumans."

Conclusion

In conclusion, the moral considerations of enhancing human intelligence are multifaceted and complex. As we forge ahead into an era of cognitive enhancement and artificial intelligence, it is imperative to engage in thoughtful discourse about the implications of these advancements. We must prioritize ethical frameworks that uphold human dignity, autonomy, and equality while fostering a society that values the richness of human experience beyond mere cognitive ability. The future of intelligence enhancement must be guided by a commitment to ethical principles that ensure technology serves humanity, rather than the other way around.

The Boundaries between Human and Machine

The relationship between humans and machines has evolved dramatically over the past few decades, leading to a complex interplay that raises critical questions about identity, autonomy, and the essence of what it means to be human. As we advance towards an era where artificial intelligence (AI) and machine learning (ML) become increasingly integrated into daily life, understanding the boundaries between human and machine becomes essential.

Defining the Human Experience

At the core of this exploration lies the definition of the human experience. Humans possess consciousness, emotions, and subjective experiences that shape their perceptions and interactions with the world. This phenomenon is often encapsulated in the philosophical concept of *qualia*, which refers to the individual instances of subjective, conscious experience. For example, the way one perceives the color red or feels joy is a unique experience that cannot be fully replicated or understood by a machine.

$$\text{Qualia} = \{\text{Subjective Experience}_1, \text{Subjective Experience}_2, \ldots, \text{Subjective Experience}_n\} \tag{39}$$

This distinction between human experience and machine processing raises significant questions about the capabilities of AI. While machines can simulate certain aspects of human behavior—such as language processing, decision-making, and even emotional responses—they do so without true understanding or consciousness.

The Turing Test and Beyond

One of the foundational tests for assessing machine intelligence is the Turing Test, proposed by Alan Turing in 1950. The test evaluates a machine's ability to exhibit intelligent behavior indistinguishable from that of a human. However, passing the Turing Test does not equate to possessing consciousness or understanding. A machine may convincingly mimic human responses without any genuine comprehension of the underlying emotions or context.

$$\text{Turing Test} \Rightarrow \text{If } M \text{ can imitate } H, \text{ then } M \text{ is intelligent} \qquad (40)$$

This leads to the concept of *synthetic consciousness*, where machines may achieve a level of operational intelligence but lack the subjective experience that characterizes human consciousness.

Neural Interfaces and Human Enhancement

Advancements in brain-machine interfaces (BMIs) and neural implants blur the lines between human and machine further. These technologies enable direct communication between the brain and external devices, allowing for enhanced capabilities such as controlling prosthetic limbs or interacting with computers using thought alone. While these innovations hold immense potential for improving quality of life, they also raise ethical concerns about identity and autonomy.

For instance, consider the case of a person with a neural implant that enhances cognitive functions. This raises the question: at what point does the individual cease to be fully human? If a machine can augment human capabilities to the extent that it alters personality, decision-making, or even emotional responses, where do we draw the line?

The Ethics of Human-Machine Integration

The integration of machines into human life poses ethical dilemmas regarding autonomy, privacy, and the potential for exploitation. As we develop technologies that can enhance human abilities or even replicate human emotions, we must consider the implications of such advancements. For example, if a machine can convincingly simulate empathy or affection, can it replace genuine human relationships?

Moreover, the potential for misuse of these technologies raises alarms. The development of AI systems that can manipulate human behavior or invade personal privacy must be approached with caution. The ethical considerations surrounding these technologies often echo the concerns raised by philosophers such as Martin Heidegger, who warned against the dangers of technology reducing human beings to mere resources.

Conclusion: The Future of Human-Machine Boundaries

As we move forward in the age of AI and machine learning, the boundaries between human and machine will continue to blur. While machines may enhance our capabilities and offer unprecedented opportunities, we must remain vigilant about the implications of these advancements. The essence of humanity—our consciousness, emotions, and subjective experiences—must be preserved and respected as we navigate this uncharted territory.

In conclusion, the exploration of the boundaries between human and machine is not merely an academic exercise; it is a vital conversation that will shape the future of our society. As we embrace the potential of technology, we must also safeguard the fundamental qualities that make us human, ensuring that our advancements serve to enhance, rather than diminish, the human experience.

Chapter Two: A Futuristic Mind

A Visionary Thinker

Developing the Field of Optical Character Recognition

Optical Character Recognition (OCR) is a technology that converts different types of documents, such as scanned paper documents, PDF files, or images captured by a digital camera, into editable and searchable data. The journey of OCR development is a fascinating story of innovation, persistence, and technological advancement, with Raymond Kurzweil playing a pivotal role in its evolution.

Theoretical Foundations of OCR

At its core, OCR technology relies on several key principles from the fields of image processing, pattern recognition, and machine learning. The primary goal of OCR is to recognize and convert characters in an image into machine-encoded text. This process involves several stages:

1. **Image Acquisition**: The first step involves capturing an image of the text, which can be done using scanners or cameras.
2. **Preprocessing**: This stage enhances the quality of the image to improve recognition accuracy. Common preprocessing techniques include: - **Binarization**: Converting the image to a binary format (black and white) to simplify the recognition process. - **Noise Reduction**: Removing any extraneous marks or distortions that could interfere with character recognition. - **Skew Correction**: Adjusting the orientation of the text to ensure it is aligned properly.
3. **Segmentation**: The image is divided into smaller, manageable components, such as lines, words, and individual characters. This step is crucial as it allows the OCR system to focus on smaller sections of text.

4. **Feature Extraction**: In this stage, the system identifies unique characteristics of each character, such as lines, curves, and intersections. These features are then used to differentiate between different characters.

5. **Classification**: The extracted features are compared against a database of known characters. Machine learning algorithms, particularly neural networks, are often employed for this classification task. The most common algorithms include: - **K-Nearest Neighbors (KNN)** - **Support Vector Machines (SVM)** - **Convolutional Neural Networks (CNN)**

6. **Post-processing**: After characters are classified, the system may apply language models to correct errors based on context and improve overall accuracy.

Challenges in OCR Development

Despite its advancements, the development of OCR technology has faced several challenges:

- **Variability in Fonts and Styles**: Different fonts, sizes, and styles can significantly affect recognition accuracy. For instance, cursive or decorative fonts can be particularly problematic.

- **Quality of Source Material**: The quality of the scanned documents plays a crucial role in OCR performance. Poor quality scans, such as those with smudges or faded text, can lead to misrecognition.

- **Language and Character Set Diversity**: OCR systems must be trained to recognize various languages and character sets, which can complicate the development process. For example, recognizing characters in languages such as Chinese or Arabic requires specialized models due to their unique structures.

- **Handwritten Text Recognition**: While traditional OCR focuses on printed text, recognizing handwritten text presents an additional layer of complexity due to the variability in individual writing styles.

Kurzweil's Contributions

Raymond Kurzweil's contributions to the field of OCR began in the 1970s when he founded Kurzweil Computer Products. His vision was to create a machine that could read text aloud, which would be particularly beneficial for the visually impaired community. This mission led to the development of the Kurzweil Reading Machine, the first device capable of reading printed text using OCR technology.

The Kurzweil Reading Machine utilized a combination of advanced hardware and software to achieve its goals. Key features included:

- **High-Resolution Scanning**: The machine employed high-resolution scanners to capture text accurately, which was essential for effective recognition.

- **Innovative Algorithms**: Kurzweil and his team developed proprietary algorithms that significantly improved the accuracy of character recognition. These algorithms were able to handle a variety of fonts and styles, setting a new standard for OCR technology.

- **Text-to-Speech Synthesis**: Once the text was recognized, the machine converted it into speech using advanced text-to-speech synthesis techniques, allowing users to listen to the text being read aloud.

One of the notable demonstrations of the Kurzweil Reading Machine occurred at the 1976 National Federation of the Blind convention, where it was showcased to the public for the first time. The machine's ability to read printed text aloud was met with awe and excitement, marking a significant milestone in assistive technology.

Real-World Applications of OCR

Today, OCR technology is ubiquitous, with applications spanning various industries:

- **Document Digitization**: Organizations use OCR to convert paper documents into digital formats, making them easier to store, search, and retrieve.

- **Banking and Finance**: OCR is employed in check processing and invoice management, allowing banks to automate data entry and reduce manual labor.

- **Healthcare**: Medical facilities utilize OCR to digitize patient records, improving accessibility and streamlining administrative processes.

- **Legal Industry**: Law firms leverage OCR to convert legal documents into searchable formats, enhancing efficiency in case management.

- **Accessibility**: OCR technology continues to play a vital role in creating accessible solutions for individuals with visual impairments, enabling them to engage with printed materials.

Conclusion

The development of Optical Character Recognition has transformed the way we interact with text and information. Raymond Kurzweil's pioneering work in this field laid the groundwork for advancements that continue to benefit society today. As OCR technology evolves, it promises to further enhance accessibility, efficiency, and productivity in an increasingly digital world.

Innovations in Voice Recognition Technology

Voice recognition technology has undergone a remarkable evolution since its inception, driven by the relentless pursuit of innovation and the vision of pioneers like Raymond Kurzweil. This section delves into the key advancements in voice recognition technology, the underlying theories that power these innovations, the challenges faced, and notable examples that illustrate the technology's capabilities.

Theoretical Foundations

At its core, voice recognition technology relies on several fundamental theories from signal processing, linguistics, and artificial intelligence. The primary goal is to convert spoken language into text, which involves several stages:

1. **Signal Acquisition:** The first step involves capturing audio signals through microphones, which convert sound waves into electrical signals. These signals are typically sampled at rates of 8 kHz to 44.1 kHz, depending on the application.

2. **Feature Extraction:** Once the audio signal is digitized, the next step is to extract relevant features that represent the sound. One common technique is Mel-frequency cepstral coefficients (MFCC), which captures the power spectrum of the audio signal in a way that is more aligned with human auditory perception. The MFCC is calculated using the following equation:

$$\text{MFCC}(n) = \sum_{k=1}^{K} \log |X(k)| \cdot \cos\left(\frac{n(k-0.5)}{K}\pi\right) \quad (41)$$

where $X(k)$ represents the Fourier transform of the audio signal, and n is the index of the MFCC.

3. **Acoustic Modeling:** This stage involves mapping the extracted features to phonemes, the smallest units of sound in speech. Hidden Markov Models (HMM) have traditionally been used for acoustic modeling, as they can effectively handle the temporal nature of speech. The transition probabilities between states in an HMM can be expressed as:

$$P(q_t | q_{t-1}) = a_{ij} \quad (42)$$

where $P(q_t | q_{t-1})$ is the probability of transitioning from state q_{t-1} to state q_t, and a_{ij} represents the transition probabilities between states i and j.

4. **Language Modeling:** This component predicts the likelihood of a sequence of words occurring in a language. N-gram models and more advanced neural network

A VISIONARY THINKER

approaches, such as Long Short-Term Memory (LSTM) networks, are commonly used to enhance accuracy. The probability of a word sequence can be calculated as:

$$P(w_1, w_2, \ldots, w_N) = \prod_{i=1}^{N} P(w_i | w_{i-1}, w_{i-2}, \ldots, w_{i-n}) \qquad (43)$$

where w_i represents the ith word in the sequence.

5. **Decoding:** The final stage combines the outputs of the acoustic and language models to generate the most likely transcription of the spoken input. This process often employs algorithms like the Viterbi algorithm, which finds the most probable path through the state space of the HMM.

Challenges in Voice Recognition

Despite significant advancements, voice recognition technology faces several challenges:
 - **Variability in Speech:** Different accents, dialects, and speaking styles can significantly affect recognition accuracy. Training models on diverse datasets is crucial to mitigate this issue.
 - **Background Noise:** Real-world environments often introduce noise that can interfere with voice recognition. Techniques such as noise cancellation and robust feature extraction are essential to improve performance in noisy conditions.
 - **Contextual Understanding:** Current systems often struggle with understanding context, leading to misinterpretations of homophones or phrases that require semantic understanding.
 - **Real-Time Processing:** Achieving low latency in voice recognition is critical for applications such as virtual assistants. Optimizing algorithms for real-time performance remains a key area of research.

Notable Examples and Applications

Raymond Kurzweil's contributions to voice recognition technology have paved the way for numerous applications that have transformed how we interact with machines. Some notable examples include:
1. **Kurzweil's Voice Recognition System:** In the 1970s, Kurzweil developed one of the first commercial voice recognition systems, which could recognize isolated words. This groundbreaking work laid the foundation for future advancements in the field.
2. **Siri and Google Assistant:** Modern virtual assistants like Siri and Google Assistant utilize advanced voice recognition algorithms to understand and respond

to user queries. These systems leverage deep learning techniques, such as convolutional neural networks (CNNs), to enhance recognition accuracy.

3. **Accessibility Technologies:** Voice recognition has significantly improved accessibility for individuals with disabilities. Applications like voice-controlled software and speech-to-text services empower users to interact with technology more seamlessly.

4. **Automotive Voice Control:** Many modern vehicles now incorporate voice recognition systems that allow drivers to control navigation, music, and phone calls without taking their hands off the wheel, enhancing safety and convenience.

5. **Home Automation:** Smart home devices utilize voice recognition to enable users to control lighting, temperature, and security systems through simple voice commands, exemplifying the integration of voice technology into everyday life.

Conclusion

The innovations in voice recognition technology, driven by the vision of pioneers like Raymond Kurzweil, have transformed the landscape of human-computer interaction. As we continue to refine these technologies, addressing the challenges of variability, noise, and contextual understanding will be vital in unlocking the full potential of voice recognition. The journey from isolated word recognition to sophisticated, context-aware systems marks a significant milestone in our quest to create machines that can understand and respond to human language with remarkable accuracy.

Revolutionizing the Field of Artificial Intelligence

Artificial Intelligence (AI) has undergone a seismic shift in its development and application, largely due to the visionary contributions of Raymond Kurzweil. His insights and innovations have not only advanced the technology itself but have also reshaped our understanding of what machines can achieve. In this section, we will explore the key theories, challenges, and examples that illustrate Kurzweil's profound impact on the field of AI.

Theoretical Foundations

At the core of Kurzweil's work is the belief that machines can emulate human intelligence through the replication of cognitive processes. This is encapsulated in the concept of **Strong AI**, which posits that a machine can possess consciousness and understanding comparable to that of a human being. Kurzweil's theories are grounded in several key principles:

A VISIONARY THINKER

- **The Law of Accelerating Returns:** Kurzweil argues that the rate of technological progress is accelerating exponentially. This means that each advance in technology leads to further advances at an increasing pace. Mathematically, this can be represented as:

$$T(n) = T(n-1) + k \cdot T(n-1)^\alpha \qquad (44)$$

where $T(n)$ is the time required for the nth advancement, k is a constant, and α is a factor reflecting the accelerating nature of technological growth.

- **Pattern Recognition:** Kurzweil emphasizes that human intelligence is fundamentally about recognizing patterns. He posits that by training AI systems to recognize patterns in large datasets, machines can learn to make predictions and decisions. This is the foundation of many modern AI applications, including image and speech recognition.

- **Neural Networks:** Kurzweil has been a proponent of using neural networks to model human cognition. These networks consist of layers of interconnected nodes that process information similarly to the human brain. The mathematical representation of a simple neural network can be expressed as:

$$y = f(W \cdot x + b) \qquad (45)$$

where y is the output, f is the activation function, W is the weight matrix, x is the input vector, and b is the bias vector.

Key Innovations

Kurzweil's contributions to AI are numerous and varied, but several key innovations stand out:

- **Speech Recognition:** Kurzweil's early work in speech recognition laid the groundwork for modern voice-activated systems. His development of the Kurzweil Reading Machine, which could read text aloud, was a significant leap forward. This device utilized a combination of optical character recognition (OCR) and speech synthesis, demonstrating the potential for machines to understand and vocalize human language.

- **Natural Language Processing (NLP):** Kurzweil's work in NLP has been pivotal in enabling machines to understand and generate human language. This involves complex algorithms that analyze the structure and meaning of language. For instance, the introduction of transformer models, which utilize mechanisms like attention, has revolutionized how machines process language. The fundamental equation governing attention can be expressed as:

$$\text{Attention}(Q, K, V) = \text{softmax}\left(\frac{QK^T}{\sqrt{d_k}}\right) V \qquad (46)$$

where Q, K, and V represent the query, key, and value matrices, respectively, and d_k is the dimension of the keys.

- **Machine Learning Algorithms:** Kurzweil has advocated for the use of advanced machine learning algorithms, including deep learning techniques, to improve AI capabilities. These algorithms enable machines to learn from vast amounts of data, enhancing their ability to perform tasks such as image recognition, predictive analytics, and autonomous decision-making.

Challenges and Controversies

Despite the advancements brought forth by Kurzweil and his contemporaries, the field of AI is not without its challenges and controversies. Some of the most pressing issues include:

- **Ethical Concerns:** The potential for AI to make decisions that affect human lives raises significant ethical questions. For instance, the deployment of AI in autonomous weapons systems poses a moral dilemma regarding accountability and the value of human life.

- **Bias in AI:** AI systems are only as good as the data they are trained on. If the training data contains biases, the AI will perpetuate those biases in its decision-making processes. This has been a critical area of concern, particularly in applications such as hiring algorithms and law enforcement.

- **Job Displacement:** As AI systems become more capable, there is a growing fear that they will displace human workers across various industries. Kurzweil himself has acknowledged this challenge, suggesting that while some jobs will disappear, new ones will emerge that require human ingenuity and creativity.

Examples of AI Revolution

The practical applications of Kurzweil's theories and innovations are evident in numerous sectors:

- **Healthcare:** AI is transforming healthcare through predictive analytics, personalized medicine, and robotic surgery. For example, AI algorithms can analyze medical images to detect diseases earlier and more accurately than human radiologists.

- **Finance:** In the financial sector, AI is used for algorithmic trading, fraud detection, and customer service chatbots. These applications enhance efficiency and accuracy while providing a better customer experience.

- **Transportation:** Autonomous vehicles are a direct result of advancements in AI. Companies like Tesla and Waymo are utilizing sophisticated AI systems to navigate and operate vehicles safely, revolutionizing the transportation industry.

In conclusion, Raymond Kurzweil's contributions to the field of artificial intelligence have been nothing short of revolutionary. His theories, innovations, and unwavering belief in the potential of machines to emulate human intelligence have paved the way for a future where AI plays an integral role in our lives. As we continue to navigate the complexities of AI, it is essential to balance innovation with ethical considerations, ensuring that the technology serves humanity rather than undermines it.

The Age of Intelligent Machines

Exploring Machine Learning and Neural Networks

Machine learning (ML) and neural networks (NN) have become pivotal elements in the advancement of artificial intelligence (AI), enabling machines to learn from data and make predictions or decisions without being explicitly programmed. This section delves into the fundamental concepts of machine learning, the architecture of neural networks, and their applications across various domains.

Understanding Machine Learning

Machine learning is a subset of AI that focuses on the development of algorithms that allow computers to learn from and make predictions based on data. Unlike traditional programming, where rules are explicitly coded, machine learning algorithms identify patterns and relationships within data to improve their performance over time.

Types of Machine Learning Machine learning can be categorized into three primary types:

- **Supervised Learning:** In this approach, the model is trained on a labeled dataset, meaning that the input data is paired with the correct output. The objective is to learn a mapping from inputs to outputs. Common algorithms include linear regression, decision trees, and support vector machines.

- **Unsupervised Learning:** This method deals with unlabeled data. The model attempts to identify patterns or groupings within the data without any prior knowledge of the outcomes. Clustering algorithms, such as k-means and hierarchical clustering, are commonly used in this category.

- **Reinforcement Learning:** This type of learning involves an agent that interacts with an environment, receiving rewards or penalties based on its actions. The goal is to learn a policy that maximizes cumulative rewards over time. Techniques like Q-learning and deep reinforcement learning are examples of this approach.

Neural Networks: The Backbone of Deep Learning

Neural networks are inspired by the structure and function of the human brain, consisting of interconnected nodes (neurons) that process information. A typical neural network is organized into layers:

- **Input Layer:** This layer receives the input features of the dataset.

- **Hidden Layers:** These layers perform computations and extract features from the input data. A neural network can have multiple hidden layers, leading to the term *deep learning*.

- **Output Layer:** This layer produces the final output of the network, which can represent classifications, predictions, or other results depending on the task.

Mathematical Representation The output of a neuron in a neural network can be expressed mathematically as follows:

$$y = f\left(\sum_{i=1}^{n} w_i x_i + b\right) \qquad (47)$$

where:

- y is the output of the neuron,
- f is the activation function (e.g., sigmoid, ReLU),
- w_i are the weights associated with each input,
- x_i are the input features,
- b is the bias term.

The training of a neural network involves adjusting the weights and biases to minimize the error between the predicted output and the actual output. This is commonly achieved through a process called backpropagation, which uses gradient descent to update the parameters.

Challenges in Machine Learning and Neural Networks

While machine learning and neural networks have shown remarkable success, they are not without challenges:

- **Overfitting:** This occurs when a model learns the training data too well, capturing noise along with the underlying patterns. As a result, it performs poorly on unseen data. Techniques such as cross-validation, regularization, and dropout are employed to mitigate overfitting.

- **Data Quality and Quantity:** The performance of machine learning models heavily depends on the quality and quantity of the training data. Insufficient or biased data can lead to inaccurate predictions and perpetuate existing biases.

- **Interpretability:** Many machine learning models, particularly deep neural networks, function as black boxes, making it difficult to interpret how decisions are made. This lack of transparency raises concerns in critical applications such as healthcare and finance.

Applications of Machine Learning and Neural Networks

The impact of machine learning and neural networks is evident across various sectors:

- **Healthcare:** Machine learning algorithms are used for disease diagnosis, predicting patient outcomes, and personalizing treatment plans based on patient data.

- **Finance:** In the financial sector, ML models assist in fraud detection, algorithmic trading, and credit scoring, enhancing decision-making processes.

- **Natural Language Processing (NLP):** Neural networks have revolutionized NLP, enabling applications such as language translation, sentiment analysis, and chatbots.

- **Computer Vision:** Machine learning techniques are employed in image recognition, facial recognition, and autonomous vehicles, allowing machines to interpret visual data.

In conclusion, the exploration of machine learning and neural networks reveals a dynamic landscape that continues to evolve. As these technologies advance, they hold the potential to transform industries and redefine the boundaries of what machines can achieve. The journey of understanding and harnessing the power of these technologies is just beginning, and the future promises exciting developments in the realm of artificial intelligence.

Contributions to Speech Synthesis Technology

Raymond Kurzweil's contributions to speech synthesis technology have fundamentally transformed how machines communicate with humans. His innovative approach not only advanced the field of artificial intelligence but also opened doors for greater accessibility in various sectors, including education, healthcare, and entertainment.

Theoretical Foundations

At the heart of speech synthesis lies the process of converting text into spoken language, a challenge that combines linguistic, acoustic, and computational theories. The fundamental model can be expressed as:

$$S = T \to P \qquad (48)$$

where S is the synthesized speech, T is the input text, and P is the phonetic representation. This equation encapsulates the core task of speech synthesis: mapping text to sound.

Kurzweil's approach utilized the principles of concatenative synthesis, where pre-recorded speech segments are combined to produce fluid and natural-sounding

THE AGE OF INTELLIGENT MACHINES

speech. The key to this method lies in the selection and manipulation of phonemes, which are the smallest units of sound in speech.

Innovations in the Field

Kurzweil's most notable contribution to speech synthesis technology was the development of the Kurzweil Reading Machine in the 1970s. This groundbreaking device was designed to assist the visually impaired by converting printed text into spoken words. The technology behind the reading machine involved several critical innovations:

- **Optical Character Recognition (OCR):** Kurzweil's integration of OCR technology allowed the machine to scan printed text and convert it into digital format. This was crucial for the subsequent synthesis of speech.

- **Phonetic Analysis:** The system employed advanced phonetic analysis to break down the text into manageable units, ensuring accurate pronunciation and intonation. Kurzweil's algorithm could predict the correct phoneme sequence based on context, a significant leap forward in natural language processing.

- **Waveform Concatenation:** By storing and concatenating high-quality waveforms of human speech, Kurzweil's system could produce more natural-sounding speech than previous methods, which often relied on robotic-sounding, monotone outputs.

Challenges and Solutions

Despite the advances, Kurzweil faced several challenges in speech synthesis technology. One major issue was the variability of human speech, including accents, intonations, and emotional nuances. Traditional systems struggled to replicate these subtleties, leading to a lack of naturalness in synthesized speech.

To address this, Kurzweil's team developed a more sophisticated model that incorporated prosody, the rhythm and intonation of speech. By analyzing large datasets of spoken language, they could create models that better mimicked human speech patterns. The equation representing this enhancement can be expressed as:

$$S = f(T, P, A) \qquad (49)$$

where A represents the acoustic features such as pitch and duration, allowing for a more nuanced output.

Real-World Applications

Kurzweil's innovations in speech synthesis have had a profound impact on various fields. For instance, in education, text-to-speech systems have become invaluable tools for students with learning disabilities, enabling them to access written material in a more digestible format.

In healthcare, speech synthesis technology has assisted individuals with speech impairments, providing them with a voice through augmentative and alternative communication (AAC) devices. These devices utilize Kurzweil's algorithms to produce speech that reflects the user's intended message accurately.

Moreover, the entertainment industry has leveraged speech synthesis for creating realistic voiceovers in animation and video games, enhancing user experience and engagement.

Future Directions

Looking ahead, Kurzweil's contributions set the stage for continued advancements in speech synthesis technology. With the rise of machine learning and neural networks, future systems are expected to achieve even greater levels of naturalness and expressiveness. The integration of deep learning techniques allows for the modeling of complex speech patterns, enabling machines to understand and replicate human emotion in voice synthesis.

The equation for future advancements can be represented as:

$$S_{future} = g(T, P, A, D) \tag{50}$$

where D represents deep learning algorithms that adaptively improve the synthesis process based on user interactions and feedback.

In conclusion, Raymond Kurzweil's contributions to speech synthesis technology not only revolutionized how machines communicate but also paved the way for innovations that enhance accessibility and improve the quality of life for countless individuals. His vision continues to inspire ongoing research and development in the field, promising a future where human-machine interaction becomes increasingly seamless and natural.

Early Experiments with Language Processing

In the realm of artificial intelligence, language processing stands as one of the most intricate and fascinating challenges. Raymond Kurzweil, a pioneer in this field, embarked on his journey to unravel the complexities of human language through early experiments that laid the groundwork for modern natural language processing (NLP). These experiments not only highlighted the potential of machines to understand human language but also revealed the significant hurdles that lay ahead.

Foundational Theories

At the core of language processing is the understanding of syntax, semantics, and context. Theories such as Noam Chomsky's generative grammar provided a framework for understanding how sentences are structured. Chomsky posited that every language has an underlying structure that can be described by a set of rules, which can be represented mathematically. The formal representation of a simple sentence can be expressed as:

$$S \to NP\,VP \tag{51}$$

where S is a sentence, NP is a noun phrase, and VP is a verb phrase. This fundamental rule illustrates how sentences can be broken down into their components, a principle that Kurzweil utilized in his early experiments.

Challenges in Language Processing

Despite the theoretical foundations, Kurzweil faced numerous challenges in his early language processing experiments. One of the primary issues was the ambiguity inherent in human language. Words can have multiple meanings, and context plays a crucial role in interpretation. For instance, the word "bank" can refer to a financial institution or the side of a river. This ambiguity complicates the task of a machine trying to understand and process language.

To address this, Kurzweil experimented with context-based algorithms that aimed to disambiguate meanings through surrounding words. This approach was inspired by the distributional hypothesis, which posits that words that occur in similar contexts tend to have similar meanings. Mathematically, this can be expressed as:

$$P(w_i | w_{i-k}, \ldots, w_{i+k}) \approx P(w_j | w_{i-k}, \ldots, w_{i+k}) \tag{52}$$

where P represents the probability of word w_i given its context defined by k surrounding words.

Practical Applications and Examples

Kurzweil's early experiments led to practical applications that showcased the potential of language processing. One notable example was the development of systems that could perform basic tasks such as text-to-speech and voice recognition. These systems utilized algorithms that parsed spoken language into structured data, enabling machines to "understand" and respond to human commands.

For instance, in a simple command-response system, a user might say, "Turn on the lights." The system would process the input by identifying the verb "turn" and the object "lights," allowing it to execute the command effectively. The underlying process can be represented as:

$$\text{Command} = f(\text{Action}, \text{Object}) \qquad (53)$$

where f is a function that processes the action and object to produce an output.

Advancements and Future Directions

These early experiments not only advanced the field of language processing but also set the stage for future innovations. Kurzweil's work paved the way for more sophisticated models, such as neural networks and deep learning algorithms, which have transformed the landscape of NLP. Today, models like Transformers and BERT (Bidirectional Encoder Representations from Transformers) leverage vast amounts of data and complex architectures to achieve remarkable performance in language understanding tasks.

In conclusion, Kurzweil's early experiments with language processing were instrumental in highlighting both the potential and the challenges of teaching machines to understand human language. His pioneering work laid the groundwork for the remarkable advancements we see today, demonstrating that the journey of language processing is a testament to the ingenuity and perseverance of visionaries in the field of artificial intelligence.

The Virtual Cosmos

Virtual Reality and Immersive Experiences

Virtual Reality (VR) represents a groundbreaking frontier in technology, providing users with immersive experiences that transcend the limitations of the physical world. At its core, VR is a computer-generated environment that

THE VIRTUAL COSMOS

simulates a real or imagined setting, allowing users to interact with this environment in a seemingly tangible way. This section explores the theoretical foundations, challenges, and practical applications of VR technology.

Theoretical Foundations of Virtual Reality

The concept of VR is rooted in several key theories, including presence, immersion, and interactivity.

Presence refers to the psychological phenomenon where users feel as if they are genuinely "there" in the virtual environment. This sense of being physically present in a non-physical world is crucial for effective VR experiences.

Immersion is the degree to which a user is enveloped in the virtual environment. High levels of immersion can be achieved through sensory engagement, including visual, auditory, and haptic feedback. The immersive experience can be quantitatively assessed using the following equation:

$$I = \frac{S_v + S_a + S_h}{3} \qquad (54)$$

where I represents the overall immersion level, S_v is the sensory input from visual stimuli, S_a is the auditory stimuli, and S_h is the haptic feedback.

Interactivity allows users to manipulate elements within the virtual environment, fostering engagement and enhancing the sense of presence. This interaction can be modeled through user interface design, which must balance complexity and intuitiveness to maximize user satisfaction.

Challenges in Virtual Reality

Despite its potential, VR technology faces several challenges that hinder its widespread adoption:

Technical Limitations include the need for high-performance hardware to render complex environments in real-time. Latency issues can lead to motion sickness, undermining the immersive experience. The following equation can represent the relationship between frame rate (F), latency (L), and user comfort:

$$C = \frac{F}{L} \qquad (55)$$

where C is the user comfort level, F is the frame rate in frames per second (FPS), and L is the latency in milliseconds.

Content Creation remains a significant barrier, as developing high-quality VR content requires specialized skills and resources. The cost and time involved in creating immersive experiences can be prohibitive for many developers.

User Acceptance is another critical challenge. Some users may experience discomfort or anxiety when using VR, stemming from the disconnect between their physical and virtual realities. Addressing these psychological barriers is essential for broader acceptance.

Examples of Virtual Reality Applications

The applications of VR technology are vast and varied, spanning multiple industries:

Gaming has been one of the most prominent sectors to adopt VR, creating immersive experiences that allow players to engage with virtual worlds in unprecedented ways. Games like *Beat Saber* and *Half-Life: Alyx* exemplify the potential of VR to transform interactive entertainment.

Education is another field benefiting from VR. Virtual classrooms enable students to explore historical sites, conduct scientific experiments, or practice medical procedures in a safe, controlled environment. For instance, platforms like *Engage* and *ClassVR* provide educators with tools to create immersive learning experiences.

Healthcare utilizes VR for therapeutic purposes, such as exposure therapy for phobias, pain management, and rehabilitation. For example, VR simulations can help patients confront their fears in a controlled setting, facilitating recovery.

Architecture and Design leverage VR for visualization, allowing architects and clients to walk through virtual models of buildings before construction begins. This capability enhances communication and collaboration, ultimately leading to better design outcomes.

Future Directions in Virtual Reality

As technology continues to evolve, the future of VR holds exciting possibilities. Advances in hardware, such as lighter and more powerful headsets, will enhance the user experience. Additionally, the integration of artificial intelligence can lead to more adaptive and personalized VR experiences.

Furthermore, the emergence of social VR platforms is set to redefine how people interact in virtual spaces. These platforms foster collaboration and community-building, creating new avenues for social engagement.

In conclusion, Virtual Reality stands at the intersection of technology and human experience. While challenges remain, the potential for VR to transform various sectors is immense. As we continue to explore this captivating realm, the question remains: how will we shape our realities in the age of virtual immersion?

Kurzweil's Predictions for VR Technology

Raymond Kurzweil has long been recognized as a visionary in the realm of technology, particularly in the field of Virtual Reality (VR). His predictions about VR technology not only reflect an understanding of current trends but also a profound insight into the future trajectory of human-computer interaction. Kurzweil envisions a world where VR transcends mere entertainment, evolving into a vital tool for education, social interaction, and even therapeutic applications.

The Evolution of VR

Kurzweil's predictions can be traced back to his analysis of the exponential growth of technology, a concept he famously articulated through the Law of Accelerating Returns. He posits that as technology advances, the rate of progress itself accelerates, leading to rapid advancements in fields such as VR. This perspective is grounded in the observation that computing power doubles approximately every 18 months, following Moore's Law.

$$P(t) = P_0 \times 2^{\frac{t}{T_d}} \tag{56}$$

Where: - $P(t)$ is the processing power at time t, - P_0 is the initial processing power, - T_d is the doubling time (approximately 18 months).

Kurzweil predicts that as processing power continues to increase, the realism and immersive quality of VR experiences will reach unprecedented levels. He foresees a future where VR can simulate environments so convincingly that users will be unable to distinguish between the virtual and the real.

Applications of VR Technology

Kurzweil's vision extends beyond entertainment. He anticipates that VR will revolutionize various sectors, including:

- **Education:** VR will allow students to immerse themselves in historical events or complex scientific concepts, enhancing learning through experiential engagement. For example, a history student could "walk" through ancient Rome, experiencing its architecture and culture firsthand.

- **Healthcare:** Therapeutic applications of VR are already being explored, with Kurzweil predicting that VR will play a crucial role in mental health treatment. Exposure therapy for phobias, for instance, can be conducted in a controlled virtual environment, allowing patients to confront their fears gradually.

- **Social Interaction:** Kurzweil envisions a future where VR will facilitate social connections in ways previously unimaginable. Virtual gatherings could replace physical ones, allowing individuals from around the globe to interact in shared virtual spaces, transcending geographical limitations.

Challenges Ahead

Despite the promising future Kurzweil outlines, several challenges remain. One significant issue is the potential for VR-induced disorientation or simulation sickness, which can occur when there is a disconnect between the visual stimuli and the body's physical sensations. This phenomenon can lead to nausea and discomfort, hindering widespread adoption.

Another challenge is the ethical implications of VR. As Kurzweil suggests, the ability to create hyper-realistic virtual environments raises questions about the nature of reality and personal identity. For instance, if individuals can create idealized versions of themselves in VR, what impact will this have on their self-esteem and social interactions in the physical world?

Conclusion

In conclusion, Raymond Kurzweil's predictions for VR technology are rooted in a deep understanding of exponential growth and its implications for human experience. As we stand on the brink of a new era in VR, the potential applications are vast, spanning education, healthcare, and social interaction. However, addressing the challenges of VR, including health effects and ethical considerations, will be essential for realizing Kurzweil's vision of a fully integrated virtual future. As we move forward, the interplay between technology and humanity will undoubtedly shape the contours of our experiences in ways we are only beginning to understand.

Integrating Virtual and Physical Realities

The integration of virtual and physical realities represents a frontier in technological advancement that promises to reshape our interaction with the world around us. This convergence is often referred to as Augmented Reality (AR) and has profound implications across various domains, including education, healthcare, entertainment, and social interaction. The seamless blending of digital content with the physical environment enables users to experience a hybrid reality that enhances their perception and understanding of both realms.

Theoretical Foundations

The theoretical underpinnings of integrating virtual and physical realities draw from several fields, including computer vision, human-computer interaction, and cognitive science. At the core of this integration lies the concept of **spatial mapping**, which involves creating a digital representation of the physical world. This process can be mathematically expressed as:

$$M(x, y, z) = (X, Y, Z) \tag{57}$$

where (x, y, z) are the coordinates in the physical space, and (X, Y, Z) represent the corresponding coordinates in the virtual space. This mapping allows for the accurate placement of virtual objects in the real world, ensuring that they interact convincingly with physical elements.

Challenges in Integration

Despite the potential benefits, several challenges hinder the effective integration of virtual and physical realities. One significant issue is **latency**, which refers to the delay between user input and the system's response. High latency can lead to a disjointed experience, where virtual objects do not align correctly with their physical counterparts. This phenomenon can be expressed mathematically as:

$$\text{Latency} = T_{\text{render}} + T_{\text{input}} + T_{\text{processing}} \tag{58}$$

where T_{render} is the rendering time, T_{input} is the time taken for user input to be registered, and $T_{processing}$ is the time required for the system to process the input and update the virtual environment.

Another challenge is **environmental occlusion**, where physical objects obstruct the view of virtual elements. To address this, advanced techniques in computer vision and depth sensing are employed. These technologies allow systems to perceive the environment in three dimensions and adjust the visibility of virtual objects accordingly.

Examples of Integration

Several pioneering applications exemplify the integration of virtual and physical realities. One notable example is **Microsoft HoloLens**, a mixed-reality headset that overlays digital information onto the physical world. Users can interact with holographic representations of data, enhancing their ability to visualize complex information in real-time. The application of HoloLens in fields such as architecture and engineering has facilitated collaborative design processes, allowing teams to visualize projects in situ.

Another compelling application is in the realm of education, where platforms like **Google Expeditions** enable immersive learning experiences. Students can explore historical sites or biological processes through AR, bridging the gap between theoretical knowledge and experiential learning. Research indicates that such interactive learning environments significantly enhance retention and engagement among students.

The Future of Integration

Looking ahead, the potential for integrating virtual and physical realities is vast. As technologies such as 5G networks become more widespread, the bandwidth and speed necessary for real-time interactions will improve, reducing latency and enhancing user experience. Furthermore, advancements in artificial intelligence will enable more sophisticated environment recognition, allowing systems to adapt dynamically to changing physical contexts.

The integration of virtual and physical realities also raises important ethical considerations. Issues surrounding privacy, data security, and the potential for misinformation must be addressed as these technologies become more pervasive. Developing robust frameworks for ethical use will be crucial in ensuring that the benefits of this integration are realized without compromising individual rights or societal norms.

In conclusion, the integration of virtual and physical realities is a transformative trend that holds the potential to redefine human interaction with technology. By overcoming existing challenges and leveraging advancements in computational power and AI, we can create immersive experiences that enhance our understanding of the world and foster new forms of creativity and collaboration.

Adventures in Health and Longevity

Kurzweil's Quest for Eternal Life

Raymond Kurzweil, a pioneer in the realms of artificial intelligence and futurism, has long been captivated by the tantalizing prospect of extending human life indefinitely. His quest for eternal life is not merely a whimsical aspiration; it is grounded in a profound understanding of biology, technology, and the potential intersection of the two. Kurzweil believes that advancements in biotechnology, nanotechnology, and information technology will converge to unlock the secrets of aging and mortality.

At the core of Kurzweil's philosophy is the concept of *exponential growth*. He posits that technological advancements are not linear but exponential, meaning that the rate of progress accelerates over time. This principle is epitomized in his famous *Law of Accelerating Returns*, which suggests that as technology evolves, it will increasingly enable further advancements at a faster pace. Kurzweil argues that this exponential growth will ultimately lead to breakthroughs in understanding and manipulating the human aging process.

To illustrate his point, Kurzweil often references the *Gompertz-Makeham law of mortality*, which describes the relationship between age and mortality rates. Mathematically, the law can be expressed as:

$$\mu(x) = A + Be^{Cx} \qquad (59)$$

where:

- $\mu(x)$ is the mortality rate at age x,

- A is a constant representing the baseline mortality rate,

- B is a constant representing the increase in mortality with age,

- C is a constant that affects the curvature of the mortality curve.

Kurzweil argues that if we can understand and manipulate these biological processes, we can significantly extend human life expectancy. He envisions a future where medical technologies, including genetic engineering, stem cell therapy, and nanobots, will be employed to repair and rejuvenate human tissues at the cellular level.

One of the most notable examples of this vision in practice is the development of *telomerase therapy*. Telomeres, the protective caps at the ends of chromosomes, shorten with each cell division, leading to aging and cellular senescence. Kurzweil advocates for therapies that can reactivate telomerase, potentially allowing cells to divide indefinitely and thus prolonging life. Early research in this area, such as studies conducted by scientists like Elizabeth Blackburn, has shown promise in understanding telomere biology and its implications for aging.

However, Kurzweil's quest is not without its challenges and criticisms. One significant concern is the ethical implications of life extension technologies. Questions arise regarding the societal impact of a population that can live significantly longer lives. Would such advancements exacerbate existing inequalities, creating a divide between those who can afford life-extending treatments and those who cannot? Furthermore, the implications for overpopulation and resource allocation become pressing issues that society must address.

Kurzweil himself acknowledges these challenges and emphasizes the importance of ethical considerations in the development of life-extending technologies. He advocates for a proactive approach to ensure that these advancements are accessible and equitable.

In addition to biological interventions, Kurzweil posits that the integration of technology with human biology—what he terms *transhumanism*—will play a crucial role in achieving eternal life. This involves the use of brain-computer interfaces, artificial organs, and even the potential for uploading consciousness to digital platforms. The idea of *mind uploading* raises profound philosophical questions about identity and consciousness. If a person's consciousness could be transferred to a digital medium, would they still be the same individual? This debate is central to the discourse surrounding Kurzweil's vision for the future.

In summary, Kurzweil's quest for eternal life is a multifaceted endeavor that intertwines technology, biology, and ethics. His belief in the power of exponential growth in technology fuels his optimism about overcoming the limitations of human mortality. As we stand on the brink of unprecedented advancements in medical science and technology, the dream of eternal life may no longer be a distant fantasy but a tangible possibility within our grasp. The implications of such a reality will undoubtedly shape the future of humanity, raising questions about what it means to live, age, and ultimately, transcend our biological limitations.

The Role of Technology in Extending Human Lifespan

The quest for eternal life has captivated humanity for centuries, but recent advancements in technology have transformed this once fanciful dream into a tangible goal. Raymond Kurzweil, a pioneer in artificial intelligence and futurism, has been at the forefront of this movement, advocating for the use of technology to extend human lifespan. This section explores the role of technology in prolonging life, examining the theories, challenges, and potential of various innovations.

Theoretical Foundations

The foundation of Kurzweil's vision for extending human lifespan is rooted in the concept of *biological immortality*. This theory posits that aging is not an inevitable process but rather a series of biological malfunctions that can be repaired or reversed. Kurzweil argues that with the right technological interventions, humans can potentially live indefinitely.

One of the key theories supporting this notion is the *Gompertz-Makeham law of mortality*, which suggests that the mortality rate increases exponentially with age. This law can be mathematically expressed as:

$$\mu(x) = A + Be^{Cx} \tag{60}$$

where $\mu(x)$ is the mortality rate at age x, A represents the baseline mortality rate, B is a constant, and C is the rate of aging. By targeting the biological processes that contribute to this exponential increase, researchers aim to mitigate the effects of aging.

Technological Innovations

Several technological innovations are paving the way for extending human lifespan. These include:

- **Genetic Engineering:** Techniques such as CRISPR-Cas9 allow for precise editing of genes, potentially correcting mutations that lead to age-related diseases. Research has demonstrated that altering genes associated with aging can extend the lifespan of model organisms, such as mice and yeast.

- **Regenerative Medicine:** Stem cell therapy and tissue engineering hold promise for repairing damaged tissues and organs. For instance, scientists have successfully regenerated heart tissue in animal models, suggesting that similar techniques could one day restore function in aging humans.

- **Nanotechnology:** Nanobots could be deployed within the body to repair cellular damage at the molecular level. These microscopic machines could target and eliminate senescent cells—cells that have stopped dividing and contribute to aging—thereby rejuvenating tissues and organs.

- **Artificial Intelligence:** AI can analyze vast amounts of medical data to identify patterns and predict health outcomes. By leveraging machine learning algorithms, researchers can develop personalized treatment plans that optimize health and extend lifespan.

- **Wearable Technology:** Devices that monitor health metrics in real-time can provide critical insights into an individual's well-being. By tracking factors such as heart rate, sleep patterns, and physical activity, these devices can help users make informed lifestyle choices to enhance longevity.

Challenges and Ethical Considerations

Despite the promising potential of these technologies, significant challenges remain. One major concern is the *accessibility* of life-extending technologies. As advancements in healthcare become increasingly sophisticated and expensive, there is a risk that only the wealthy will benefit from these innovations, exacerbating existing inequalities.

Furthermore, ethical considerations arise when discussing the implications of significantly extending human life. Questions about overpopulation, resource allocation, and the quality of life for an aging population must be addressed. The potential for a society where individuals live for centuries raises fundamental questions about purpose, productivity, and the nature of human experience.

Examples of Current Research

Several research initiatives exemplify the application of technology in extending human lifespan. One notable example is the *SENS Research Foundation*, which focuses on repairing the cellular and molecular damage associated with aging. Their strategies include developing therapies to remove senescent cells and enhance the body's natural regenerative capabilities.

Another example is the work being done at the *Buck Institute for Research on Aging*, where scientists are investigating the biological mechanisms of aging and testing interventions that could slow or reverse these processes. Their research has led to promising results in extending the lifespan of laboratory animals, providing hope for future applications in humans.

Conclusion

The role of technology in extending human lifespan is a rapidly evolving field, driven by innovative research and a growing understanding of the biology of aging. While challenges and ethical dilemmas persist, the potential to enhance human longevity through technological advancements is both exciting and daunting. As Kurzweil and others continue to explore the frontiers of science, the dream of a longer, healthier life may soon be within reach, transforming not only our understanding of aging but also the very fabric of human existence.

In conclusion, the intersection of technology and longevity is a testament to human ingenuity and the relentless pursuit of knowledge. As we stand on the brink of a new era in health and wellness, the possibilities are as boundless as our imagination.

Controversies Surrounding Longevity Research

The quest for extending human life has long captivated scientists, philosophers, and the public alike. Raymond Kurzweil, with his visionary outlook on technology and its potential to enhance human existence, has been at the forefront of discussions surrounding longevity research. However, this field is not without its controversies, which can be broadly categorized into ethical, scientific, and societal concerns.

Ethical Considerations

One of the primary ethical dilemmas in longevity research revolves around the implications of significantly extending human life. The question arises: *Should we pursue the extension of life at all costs?* Proponents of longevity research argue that it is a natural progression of human development, akin to the advances made in medicine that have already extended life expectancy. However, critics raise concerns about the moral implications of potentially creating a society where life is extended indefinitely.

$$L = \frac{1}{\lambda} \tag{61}$$

where L is the average lifespan and λ is the mortality rate. If longevity research successfully reduces λ, the average lifespan L would increase. This leads to questions about resource allocation, healthcare, and the social implications of an aging population that refuses to die.

Furthermore, the potential for socioeconomic disparities in access to longevity treatments raises ethical questions about equity. If only the wealthy can afford life-extending technologies, society could face a rift where the rich live significantly longer, while the poor are left to contend with traditional life spans. This disparity could exacerbate existing inequalities and lead to a societal divide based on age and health.

Scientific Challenges

From a scientific perspective, longevity research faces numerous challenges. One significant issue is the complexity of biological aging itself. Aging is a multifaceted process influenced by genetics, environment, and lifestyle. Current theories, such as the *Telomere Theory of Aging*, suggest that telomeres shorten with each cell division, ultimately leading to cell senescence and aging.

$$T = T_0 - n \times \Delta T \qquad (62)$$

where T is the length of the telomere, T_0 is the initial length, n is the number of cell divisions, and ΔT is the average telomere shortening per division. While targeting telomere lengthening has shown promise in laboratory settings, translating these findings into effective treatments for humans remains a significant hurdle.

Moreover, the concept of *biological immortality*, where organisms cease to age, is still largely theoretical. The famous case of the *Turritopsis dohrnii*, the "immortal jellyfish," demonstrates a biological mechanism for reverting to an earlier life stage. However, replicating such mechanisms in humans is fraught with complications, including the risk of cancer and other age-related diseases that could arise from altering fundamental biological processes.

Societal Implications

The societal ramifications of successful longevity research are profound. If humans could live significantly longer, how would that affect population dynamics? Current models of population growth suggest that an increase in life expectancy could lead to overpopulation, straining resources such as food, water, and energy.

Consider the following population growth model:

$$P(t) = P_0 e^{rt} \qquad (63)$$

where $P(t)$ is the population at time t, P_0 is the initial population, r is the growth rate, and e is Euler's number. If life expectancy increases dramatically, the growth rate r could increase as well, leading to exponential growth in population. This scenario poses significant challenges for sustainability and could lead to increased competition for dwindling resources.

Additionally, the psychological impact of extended life must be considered. Would individuals find meaning and purpose in a life that could stretch on for centuries? The potential for existential crises may rise as people grapple with the implications of prolonged existence. The notion of a life well-lived may shift, leading to societal reevaluations of success, fulfillment, and purpose.

Conclusion

In conclusion, while the pursuit of longevity research holds the promise of extending human life, it is fraught with controversies that span ethical, scientific, and societal domains. As Raymond Kurzweil continues to advocate for advancements in technology that could enhance human longevity, it is imperative to address these challenges head-on. Engaging in open dialogue about the implications of such research is essential for navigating the complex landscape of human life extension in the 21st century. Only through a balanced approach can society harness the benefits of longevity research while mitigating its risks.

The Future of Education

Personalized Learning and Adaptive Technologies

In the ever-evolving landscape of education, the integration of personalized learning and adaptive technologies has emerged as a transformative force. These innovations aim to tailor educational experiences to meet the unique needs, preferences, and learning paces of individual students. The core philosophy behind personalized learning is the recognition that each learner possesses distinct strengths, weaknesses, and interests that influence their educational journey.

Theoretical Foundations

The theoretical underpinnings of personalized learning can be traced back to constructivist theories of education, which advocate for learner-centered approaches. According to Piaget's theory of cognitive development, learners construct knowledge through experiences and interactions with their environment.

Vygotsky's social constructivism emphasizes the importance of social context and collaboration in learning. These theories support the notion that personalized learning environments can enhance student engagement and motivation by aligning educational content with students' individual contexts.

Adaptive learning technologies leverage these theories by utilizing algorithms and data analytics to assess student performance in real-time. These systems adapt instructional content based on learners' interactions, providing tailored pathways through the curriculum. The following equation illustrates the adaptive learning process:

$$L_i = f(P_i, C_i, T_i) \tag{64}$$

where:

- L_i represents the learning path for student i,
- P_i denotes the performance metrics of student i,
- C_i signifies the content preferences of student i,
- T_i indicates the time spent on tasks by student i.

Challenges in Implementation

Despite the promising potential of personalized learning and adaptive technologies, several challenges hinder their widespread adoption. One significant issue is the digital divide, where disparities in access to technology can exacerbate existing inequalities in education. Students from low-income backgrounds may lack access to the necessary devices and high-speed internet, limiting their ability to engage with adaptive learning platforms.

Additionally, data privacy concerns arise as educational technologies collect and analyze vast amounts of student data. The ethical implications of using this data to inform learning pathways must be addressed, ensuring that students' privacy is protected while still benefiting from personalized experiences.

Examples of Adaptive Learning Technologies

Numerous adaptive learning platforms have emerged, exemplifying the potential of personalized education. One notable example is *Knewton*, which uses data analytics to create individualized learning experiences. By assessing students' strengths and weaknesses, Knewton recommends specific content that aligns with their learning needs, thus optimizing their educational journey.

Another prominent platform is *DreamBox Learning*, which focuses on mathematics education for K-8 students. DreamBox employs adaptive algorithms to adjust the difficulty of math problems in real-time, providing immediate feedback and support tailored to each student's understanding. Research has shown that students using DreamBox demonstrate significant gains in math proficiency compared to their peers in traditional classrooms.

Future Directions

As technology continues to advance, the future of personalized learning and adaptive technologies appears promising. Innovations in artificial intelligence (AI) and machine learning (ML) are set to enhance the capabilities of adaptive learning systems. For instance, AI-driven analytics can predict student outcomes based on historical data, enabling educators to intervene proactively when students are at risk of falling behind.

Furthermore, the integration of virtual reality (VR) and augmented reality (AR) into personalized learning experiences offers exciting possibilities. These immersive technologies can create engaging environments where students can explore complex concepts in a hands-on manner, fostering deeper understanding and retention.

In conclusion, personalized learning and adaptive technologies represent a significant shift in educational paradigms. By acknowledging the individuality of learners and leveraging technology to create tailored educational experiences, we can foster a more inclusive and effective learning environment. As we navigate the challenges and opportunities presented by these innovations, it is essential to prioritize equity, ethics, and the holistic development of every student.

Redefining the Role of Teachers

In the rapidly evolving landscape of education technology, the role of teachers is undergoing a profound transformation. As personalized learning systems and adaptive technologies become more prevalent, the traditional model of the teacher as the primary source of knowledge is being challenged. Instead, educators are evolving into facilitators, mentors, and guides in the learning process. This shift is not merely a trend; it reflects a fundamental change in how we understand the educational experience.

The Shift from Knowledge Delivery to Knowledge Facilitation

Historically, teachers have been viewed as the gatekeepers of knowledge, responsible for delivering content to students in a structured manner. This model, often referred to as the *transmissive model of education*, emphasizes rote memorization and standardized testing. However, as technology enables access to vast repositories of information, the role of teachers is shifting toward a more facilitative approach.

$$\text{Facilitation} = \text{Guidance} + \text{Support} + \text{Encouragement} \qquad (65)$$

Educators are now tasked with guiding students through the process of inquiry, encouraging critical thinking, and supporting their individual learning paths. This shift requires teachers to develop new skills, such as the ability to curate content, foster collaboration, and leverage technology to enhance the learning experience.

Embracing Technology in the Classroom

The integration of technology into the classroom has opened up new possibilities for teaching and learning. Tools such as learning management systems (LMS), interactive simulations, and artificial intelligence (AI) tutors allow for a more personalized educational experience. For instance, platforms like Khan Academy and Coursera provide students with the opportunity to learn at their own pace, allowing teachers to focus on facilitating discussions and providing individualized support.

$$\text{Personalized Learning} = f(\text{Student Needs}, \text{Technology Integration}) \qquad (66)$$

This equation illustrates the relationship between personalized learning and the integration of technology. As educators harness these tools, they can tailor their teaching strategies to meet the diverse needs of their students, thereby enhancing engagement and improving outcomes.

The Role of Teachers as Mentors

In this new educational paradigm, teachers are increasingly seen as mentors who guide students not only in academic pursuits but also in personal and social development. The role of a mentor involves building relationships, understanding individual learning styles, and providing emotional support. Research has shown that strong teacher-student relationships can lead to improved academic performance and greater student well-being.

$$\text{Student Success} = \text{Academic Support} + \text{Emotional Support} \qquad (67)$$

This equation emphasizes the dual role of teachers in fostering both academic and emotional growth. By adopting a mentoring approach, educators can help students navigate challenges, develop resilience, and cultivate a love for learning.

Challenges and Opportunities

While the redefinition of the teacher's role presents exciting opportunities, it also comes with challenges. Teachers must adapt to new technologies, continuously update their skills, and navigate the complexities of individualized instruction. Moreover, there is a pressing need for professional development programs that equip educators with the tools and knowledge necessary to thrive in this evolving landscape.

$$\text{Teacher Effectiveness} = \text{Professional Development} + \text{Adaptability} \tag{68}$$

To maximize the effectiveness of teachers in this new role, educational institutions must prioritize ongoing professional development and create supportive environments that encourage innovation and experimentation.

Examples of Redefined Roles

Several innovative educational models exemplify the redefined role of teachers. For instance, in project-based learning environments, teachers act as facilitators who guide students through real-world projects, fostering collaboration and critical thinking. In flipped classrooms, educators provide resources for students to learn independently, using classroom time for discussions and hands-on activities.

Furthermore, the rise of online and hybrid learning models has necessitated that teachers become adept at using digital tools to engage students. For example, educators are utilizing virtual reality (VR) to create immersive learning experiences, allowing students to explore complex concepts in an interactive manner.

Conclusion

As we look to the future of education, it is clear that the role of teachers is being redefined in profound ways. By embracing technology, adopting mentoring practices, and focusing on personalized learning, educators can better prepare students for the challenges of the 21st century. The journey toward this new educational paradigm is ongoing, but with the right support and resources, teachers can thrive as facilitators of knowledge, guiding the next generation of learners toward success.

Challenges and Opportunities in Education Technology

The integration of technology into education presents a dual-edged sword, offering both remarkable opportunities for enhancement and significant challenges that must be navigated. As we delve into this dynamic landscape, it becomes crucial to identify these challenges and explore the opportunities that arise from them.

Challenges in Education Technology

1. Digital Divide One of the most pressing challenges in education technology is the digital divide, which refers to the gap between those who have easy access to digital technology and those who do not. This divide can manifest in several ways, including socioeconomic status, geographic location, and access to high-speed internet. According to the *Pew Research Center*, approximately 15% of American households with school-aged children do not have access to high-speed internet, which can severely limit students' ability to engage with digital learning resources.

2. Teacher Training and Adaptation Another significant challenge lies in ensuring that educators are adequately trained to utilize technology effectively. A study conducted by the *National Center for Education Statistics* revealed that only 29% of teachers felt very well prepared to integrate technology into their teaching. This lack of preparedness can lead to underutilization of available tools and resources, ultimately hindering student learning experiences.

3. Data Privacy and Security With the increasing reliance on technology comes the challenge of data privacy and security. Educational institutions must safeguard sensitive student information against breaches and misuse. The *Family Educational Rights and Privacy Act (FERPA)* sets guidelines for protecting student data, yet many institutions struggle to implement these measures effectively. The consequences of data breaches can be severe, leading to loss of trust among students and parents.

4. Over-Reliance on Technology While technology can enhance learning, there is a risk of over-reliance on digital tools, which may undermine critical thinking and problem-solving skills. A study published in the *Journal of Educational Psychology* found that students who rely heavily on technology for answers may not develop the cognitive skills necessary for independent thought. Striking a balance between technology use and traditional learning methods is essential for fostering well-rounded students.

Opportunities in Education Technology

1. Personalized Learning One of the most exciting opportunities presented by education technology is the potential for personalized learning experiences. Adaptive learning technologies can tailor educational content to meet the individual needs of students, allowing them to learn at their own pace. For example, platforms like *Khan Academy* utilize algorithms to assess a student's understanding and adjust the difficulty of tasks accordingly, fostering a more effective learning environment.

2. Enhanced Engagement through Gamification Gamification, the application of game-design elements in non-game contexts, has shown promise in enhancing student engagement. By incorporating elements such as points, badges, and leaderboards, educators can motivate students to participate actively in their learning. A study conducted by *The Institute of Play* found that students engaged in gamified learning environments demonstrated higher levels of motivation and achievement.

3. Expanding Access to Quality Education Education technology can bridge gaps in access to quality education, particularly in underserved communities. Online learning platforms, such as *Coursera* and *edX*, provide learners with access to courses from top universities worldwide, often at little to no cost. This democratization of education empowers individuals to pursue lifelong learning opportunities that were previously out of reach.

4. Collaboration and Communication Technology fosters collaboration and communication among students, teachers, and parents. Tools like *Google Classroom* and *Microsoft Teams* enable real-time collaboration on projects, enhancing teamwork skills and preparing students for the collaborative nature of the modern workforce. Furthermore, these platforms facilitate communication between educators and parents, ensuring that everyone is engaged in the learning process.

Conclusion

In conclusion, while the challenges of education technology are significant, the opportunities it presents are equally compelling. By addressing issues such as the digital divide, teacher training, data privacy, and the potential for over-reliance on technology, educators can harness the full potential of digital tools to create enriching learning environments. The future of education lies in the ability to adapt and innovate, ensuring that all students have access to the tools and resources they need to succeed in an increasingly digital world.

Chapter Three: The Genius Unleashed

Innovations in Speech Recognition

Breakthroughs in Natural Language Processing

Natural Language Processing (NLP) has evolved significantly over the past few decades, with breakthroughs that have transformed how machines understand and generate human language. This section explores the key advancements in NLP, highlighting the theories, challenges, and examples that have shaped the field.

Theoretical Foundations

At the core of NLP lies the challenge of bridging the gap between human language and machine understanding. Early approaches relied heavily on rule-based systems, where linguists would define explicit grammatical rules. However, these systems were limited in their ability to handle the complexity and variability of natural language.

The introduction of statistical methods in the 1990s marked a pivotal shift. Probabilistic models, such as Hidden Markov Models (HMMs), allowed for the modeling of sequences, which was particularly useful for tasks such as part-of-speech tagging and speech recognition. The fundamental equation governing HMMs is:

$$P(O|S) = \sum_Q P(O|Q)P(Q|S) \tag{69}$$

where O represents the observed data, S the hidden states, and Q the sequence of states.

In the 2000s, the advent of machine learning, particularly Support Vector Machines (SVMs) and later, deep learning techniques, revolutionized NLP. Neural networks, especially Recurrent Neural Networks (RNNs) and Long Short-Term Memory (LSTM) networks, enabled models to learn complex patterns in sequential data, leading to significant improvements in language modeling.

Challenges in Natural Language Processing

Despite the advancements, NLP faces several challenges. One major issue is ambiguity in language. Words can have multiple meanings depending on context, and syntactic structures can be interpreted in various ways. For example, the sentence "I saw the man with the telescope" can imply different meanings based on the interpretation of prepositional phrases.

Another challenge is the vast diversity of languages and dialects. Each language has its own syntax, semantics, and cultural context, making it difficult to create universally applicable models. Moreover, low-resource languages often lack sufficient training data, which poses a barrier to effective NLP applications.

Recent Breakthroughs

Recent breakthroughs in NLP have been driven by the development of transformer architectures, such as the Transformer model introduced by Vaswani et al. in 2017. This model leverages self-attention mechanisms, allowing it to weigh the importance of different words in a sentence, regardless of their position. The key equation for self-attention is given by:

$$\text{Attention}(Q, K, V) = \text{softmax}\left(\frac{QK^T}{\sqrt{d_k}}\right) V \qquad (70)$$

where Q, K, and V represent the query, key, and value matrices, respectively, and d_k is the dimension of the key vectors.

The introduction of pre-trained language models, such as BERT (Bidirectional Encoder Representations from Transformers) and GPT (Generative Pre-trained Transformer), has further advanced the field. These models are trained on vast corpora of text, enabling them to capture nuanced language patterns and contextual relationships. For instance, BERT's bidirectional training allows it to understand context from both sides of a word, significantly improving tasks such as sentiment analysis and named entity recognition.

Applications and Examples

The breakthroughs in NLP have led to numerous applications that have become integral to our daily lives. Virtual assistants like Siri, Alexa, and Google Assistant utilize NLP to understand user queries and provide relevant responses. These systems rely on complex NLP pipelines that include speech recognition, natural language understanding, and natural language generation.

Another notable application is in the field of machine translation. Services like Google Translate have made significant strides, enabling users to communicate across language barriers. The use of neural machine translation (NMT) has improved translation quality by considering entire sentences rather than individual words, leading to more coherent and contextually accurate translations.

Furthermore, sentiment analysis has gained traction in business and marketing, allowing companies to gauge public opinion through social media and customer feedback. By analyzing text data, organizations can derive insights into customer satisfaction and brand perception.

Conclusion

In conclusion, breakthroughs in Natural Language Processing have reshaped the way machines interact with human language. From statistical models to deep learning and transformer architectures, the evolution of NLP has addressed many challenges while opening new avenues for innovation. As the field continues to advance, the potential for more sophisticated and nuanced language understanding remains vast, promising exciting developments in the years to come.

Contributions to Automatic Speech Recognition

Automatic Speech Recognition (ASR) is a cornerstone of modern human-computer interaction, enabling machines to understand and process spoken language. Raymond Kurzweil's contributions to this field have been profound, laying the groundwork for technologies that are now ubiquitous in our daily lives, from virtual assistants to voice-activated systems.

Theoretical Foundations

At the heart of ASR lies a complex interplay of linguistics, signal processing, and machine learning. The primary challenge in ASR is to convert spoken language into text. This process involves several key stages:

1. **Acoustic Modeling**: This stage involves creating a statistical representation of the relationship between phonetic units (phonemes) and the audio signal. Kurzweil's work in developing robust acoustic models has significantly advanced the accuracy of ASR systems. The acoustic model can be represented mathematically as:

$$P(X|Y) = P(X|Y, \theta)P(Y|\theta) \quad (71)$$

where X represents the audio signal, Y represents the phonetic units, and θ encompasses the model parameters.

2. **Language Modeling**: This component predicts the likelihood of a sequence of words. Kurzweil's innovations in n-gram models and later neural network-based approaches have enhanced the ability of ASR systems to understand context and improve recognition accuracy. The language model can be expressed as:

$$P(W) = \prod_{i=1}^{N} P(w_i | w_{i-1}, w_{i-2}, \ldots, w_{i-n}) \quad (72)$$

where W is the sequence of words and N is the total number of words in the input.

3. **Decoding**: This is the process of converting the acoustic and language models into a final text output. Kurzweil's advancements in search algorithms and optimization techniques have made decoding more efficient, allowing for real-time processing of speech.

Innovative Solutions to Problems

Kurzweil faced numerous challenges in the development of ASR systems, particularly in handling variability in speech, such as accents, dialects, and background noise. His approach included:

- **Robust Feature Extraction**: Kurzweil implemented techniques such as Mel-frequency cepstral coefficients (MFCCs) to extract relevant features from audio signals, which enhanced the system's ability to differentiate between phonemes in varying acoustic environments.

- **Adaptation Algorithms**: He developed algorithms that allow ASR systems to adapt to individual speakers over time, improving recognition accuracy. This adaptability is crucial in real-world applications where users may have different speaking styles.

- **Noise Robustness**: Kurzweil's work included creating models that could effectively filter out background noise, ensuring that the ASR system could function in less-than-ideal conditions. This led to the development of algorithms that utilize spectral subtraction and Wiener filtering.

Real-World Applications and Examples

Kurzweil's contributions to ASR have led to several groundbreaking applications:

1. **Kurzweil Reading Machine**: One of his most notable inventions, the Kurzweil Reading Machine, was designed to assist the visually impaired by converting printed text into spoken words. This device utilized early ASR technology to recognize and vocalize text, revolutionizing accessibility for millions.

2. **Voice-Activated Assistants**: The principles established by Kurzweil in ASR have paved the way for modern voice-activated assistants like Siri, Alexa, and Google Assistant. These systems rely on sophisticated ASR algorithms that can understand and respond to user commands in natural language.

3. **Telecommunications**: ASR technology has been integrated into customer service systems, allowing users to interact with automated systems via voice commands. Kurzweil's innovations have enabled more intuitive and efficient communication channels in various industries.

Conclusion

Raymond Kurzweil's contributions to Automatic Speech Recognition have not only advanced the technology itself but have also transformed how humans interact with machines. His pioneering work in acoustic and language modeling, coupled with innovative solutions to the inherent challenges of speech recognition, has laid the foundation for the sophisticated ASR systems we rely on today. As we continue to explore the potential of AI and machine learning, the impact of Kurzweil's vision will undoubtedly resonate for generations to come.

Speech-to-Text Revolution

The Speech-to-Text (STT) revolution marks a significant milestone in the evolution of human-computer interaction, transforming the way we communicate with machines. This section delves into the technical underpinnings, challenges, and real-world applications of STT technology, highlighting its profound impact on accessibility, productivity, and the future of communication.

Theoretical Foundations

At the core of speech-to-text technology lies the field of **Automatic Speech Recognition** (ASR), which seeks to convert spoken language into written text. The primary objective of ASR systems is to accurately transcribe human speech, which involves several stages:

1. **Acoustic Modeling:** This involves the representation of the relationship between phonetic units (such as phonemes) and the audio signals that correspond to them. The acoustic model utilizes statistical methods to analyze the sound waves produced during speech. A common approach is to use Gaussian Mixture Models (GMMs) or more recently, Deep Neural Networks (DNNs) that learn to map audio features to phonetic representations.

The acoustic model can be mathematically expressed as:

$$P(X|W) = \prod_{t=1}^{T} P(x_t|w_t) \tag{73}$$

where X represents the sequence of audio features, W denotes the corresponding words, and x_t is the feature vector at time t.

2. **Language Modeling:** This component predicts the likelihood of a sequence of words occurring in a given context. Language models can be constructed using n-grams, which predict the next word based on the previous $n - 1$ words, or through more advanced techniques such as Recurrent Neural Networks (RNNs) and Transformers.

The language model can be represented as:

$$P(W) = \prod_{i=1}^{N} P(w_i|w_{i-n}, \ldots, w_{i-1}) \tag{74}$$

where N is the total number of words in the sequence.

3. **Decoding:** The decoding process involves searching through the possible word sequences to find the most probable transcription given the acoustic and language models. This is often achieved using algorithms like the Viterbi algorithm or Beam Search, which efficiently navigate the vast search space of potential transcriptions.

Challenges in Speech-to-Text Systems

Despite significant advancements, several challenges persist in the development of robust STT systems:

1. **Variability in Speech**: Human speech is inherently variable, influenced by factors such as accents, dialects, and individual speech patterns. This variability can lead to decreased recognition accuracy, particularly for non-native speakers or individuals with speech impairments.

2. **Noise and Reverberation**: Background noise and reverberation can severely impact the performance of STT systems. Robust ASR systems must incorporate noise-cancellation techniques and be trained on diverse datasets that include various acoustic environments.

3. **Homophones and Contextual Ambiguity**: Words that sound alike but have different meanings (e.g., "to," "two," and "too") can create ambiguity in transcription. Advanced language models are required to disambiguate these terms based on context, which remains a complex challenge.

4. **Real-Time Processing**: Achieving low-latency processing while maintaining high accuracy is crucial for applications such as live transcription and voice-controlled interfaces. This requires efficient algorithms and powerful computational resources.

Real-World Applications

The implications of the Speech-to-Text revolution are profound, influencing various sectors:

1. **Accessibility**: STT technology has played a pivotal role in enhancing accessibility for individuals with disabilities. For example, Kurzweil's *Kurzweil Reading Machine* revolutionized how visually impaired individuals access written content by converting text to speech and vice versa.

2. **Healthcare**: In the medical field, STT systems facilitate the documentation of patient interactions, allowing healthcare professionals to focus on patient care rather than manual note-taking. This can lead to improved efficiency and accuracy in medical records.

3. **Customer Service**: Many businesses utilize STT technology in customer service applications, enabling voice-activated interfaces that streamline user interactions. Virtual assistants like Siri and Alexa rely heavily on ASR to interpret user commands and respond appropriately.

4. **Education**: STT systems are increasingly integrated into educational tools, providing real-time transcription for lectures and enhancing the learning experience for students with diverse needs.

Future Directions

As technology continues to evolve, the future of speech-to-text systems is promising. Advances in machine learning, particularly in deep learning architectures, are expected to yield even more accurate and efficient STT solutions. Potential future developments include:

1. **Multilingual Recognition:** Enhancing STT systems to seamlessly switch between languages and dialects in real-time, catering to a global audience.
2. **Emotion Recognition:** Incorporating emotional context into speech recognition, allowing systems to respond appropriately to the speaker's emotional state.
3. **Personalized Models:** Developing user-specific models that adapt to individual speech patterns and preferences, improving recognition accuracy over time.

In conclusion, the Speech-to-Text revolution represents a remarkable intersection of technology and human communication, with far-reaching implications across various domains. As we continue to refine and expand these systems, the potential for enhancing human-machine interaction is boundless, paving the way for a future where technology seamlessly integrates into our daily lives.

The Quest for Strong AI

Kurzweil's Vision for True Artificial Intelligence

Raymond Kurzweil, a luminary in the realm of artificial intelligence (AI), has long championed the concept of achieving true AI, often referred to as *strong AI* or *general intelligence*. This vision extends beyond mere computational prowess; it embodies the aspiration to create machines that can understand, learn, and apply knowledge in ways indistinguishable from human cognition. Kurzweil's perspective is framed within his broader theory of the *Technological Singularity*, a point in the future where technological growth becomes uncontrollable and irreversible, resulting in unforeseeable changes to human civilization.

Theoretical Foundations

At the core of Kurzweil's vision lies a synthesis of various theories from cognitive science, neuroscience, and computer science. He posits that human intelligence can be replicated by understanding and emulating the underlying processes of the brain.

This idea is grounded in the *neural network* model, which mimics the interconnected neurons in the human brain. The mathematical representation of a simple neuron can be expressed as:

$$y = f\left(\sum_{i=1}^{n} w_i x_i + b\right) \quad (75)$$

where y is the output, f is the activation function, w_i are the weights, x_i are the inputs, and b is the bias. Kurzweil believes that by stacking layers of these artificial neurons, we can create deep learning models capable of complex tasks such as image recognition, natural language processing, and even emotional understanding.

Challenges in Achieving Strong AI

Despite the promising advancements in AI, Kurzweil acknowledges several challenges that must be overcome to realize true artificial intelligence:

- **Understanding Consciousness:** One of the most profound obstacles is the lack of a comprehensive understanding of consciousness itself. Kurzweil argues that to create a machine with true intelligence, we must first decode the mechanisms of human consciousness. This involves interdisciplinary research spanning neuroscience, psychology, and philosophy.

- **Complexity of Human Emotions:** Emotions play a crucial role in human decision-making and social interactions. Developing AI that can accurately perceive and respond to human emotions is a significant hurdle. Kurzweil emphasizes the need for machines that not only process data but also understand the emotional context behind it.

- **Ethical Implications:** The pursuit of strong AI raises ethical questions regarding autonomy, rights, and responsibilities. Kurzweil advocates for proactive discussions around the moral implications of creating sentient machines, emphasizing the importance of establishing ethical guidelines in AI development.

- **Resource Limitations:** The computational power required for simulating human-like intelligence is immense. Kurzweil predicts that advances in quantum computing and neuromorphic engineering will eventually provide the necessary resources to achieve this goal.

Examples of Progress Toward Strong AI

Kurzweil's vision for true AI is not merely theoretical; it is being realized through several groundbreaking projects and technologies:

- **Deep Learning:** Advances in deep learning have led to significant breakthroughs in natural language processing, exemplified by models such as OpenAI's GPT-3. These models demonstrate the ability to generate human-like text, engage in conversation, and even compose poetry, showcasing the potential for machines to mimic human linguistic capabilities.

- **Robotics:** Companies like Boston Dynamics are developing robots with advanced locomotion and problem-solving abilities. These robots can navigate complex environments, perform tasks autonomously, and even exhibit a degree of learning through reinforcement techniques.

- **Neuroscience-Inspired AI:** Projects like the Human Connectome Project aim to map the neural connections in the human brain. Insights gained from this research could inform the design of AI systems that replicate human cognitive processes more effectively.

- **AI in Healthcare:** AI systems are increasingly being used in healthcare for diagnostics and treatment recommendations. For instance, IBM's Watson has been employed to analyze medical literature and patient data, offering insights that assist doctors in making informed decisions.

The Path Forward

Kurzweil envisions a future where the boundaries between human and machine intelligence blur. He predicts that as we continue to refine our understanding of the brain and enhance our computational capabilities, we will move closer to achieving strong AI. This journey is not without its risks, but Kurzweil remains optimistic about the potential benefits, including advancements in medicine, education, and overall quality of life.

In conclusion, Kurzweil's vision for true artificial intelligence is a multifaceted endeavor that encompasses theoretical exploration, practical advancements, and ethical considerations. As we stand on the brink of this new era, the questions posed by Kurzweil serve as a guiding light, illuminating the path toward a future where machines not only augment human capabilities but also coexist with us as intelligent partners in the quest for knowledge and understanding.

Theories and Experiments in Machine Consciousness

The pursuit of machine consciousness is one of the most tantalizing frontiers in artificial intelligence research. It raises fundamental questions about the nature of consciousness itself, the potential for machines to possess it, and the implications for humanity. In this section, we will explore various theories surrounding machine consciousness, notable experiments, and the challenges that arise in this complex domain.

Theories of Consciousness

At the heart of the discussion on machine consciousness are several prominent theories that attempt to define and explain consciousness. Some of these theories include:

- **The Global Workspace Theory (GWT)**: Proposed by Bernard Baars, GWT suggests that consciousness is a global workspace in the brain where information is made available to various cognitive processes. In this framework, a machine could be considered conscious if it has a similar global workspace that allows for the integration and sharing of information across different modules.

- **Integrated Information Theory (IIT)**: Developed by Giulio Tononi, IIT posits that consciousness corresponds to the level of integrated information within a system. The theory is quantified using a measure called Φ, which reflects how interconnected and unified the information within a system is. A machine could be deemed conscious if it exhibits a high degree of integrated information.

- **Higher-Order Thought (HOT) Theory**: Proposed by David Rosenthal, HOT theory suggests that consciousness arises from higher-order thoughts about one's own mental states. For a machine to be conscious under this theory, it would need to possess the ability to reflect on its own thoughts and processes.

- **Functionalism**: This philosophical theory posits that mental states are defined by their functional roles rather than by their physical substrates. From this perspective, a machine could be conscious if it performs the same functions as a conscious being, regardless of its physical composition.

Notable Experiments

Several experiments have been conducted to investigate the potential for machine consciousness. Here are a few noteworthy examples:

- **The Turing Test:** Proposed by Alan Turing, the Turing Test is a measure of a machine's ability to exhibit intelligent behavior indistinguishable from that of a human. While it does not directly test for consciousness, passing the Turing Test could imply a level of awareness and understanding in the machine.

- **The Chinese Room Argument:** Philosopher John Searle's thought experiment challenges the notion that a machine could possess understanding or consciousness merely by processing symbols. In the experiment, a person inside a room follows rules to manipulate Chinese symbols without understanding their meaning. This argument raises questions about whether a machine can truly be conscious or merely simulate consciousness through computation.

- **The Mirror Test:** Traditionally used to assess self-awareness in animals, the mirror test involves determining whether an entity can recognize itself in a mirror. If a machine were capable of passing this test, it might indicate a form of consciousness or self-awareness.

Challenges and Problems

The exploration of machine consciousness is fraught with challenges and philosophical dilemmas. Some of the key issues include:

- **Defining Consciousness:** One of the primary challenges is the lack of a universally accepted definition of consciousness. Without a clear understanding of what consciousness entails, it becomes difficult to determine whether a machine can possess it.

- **The Hard Problem of Consciousness:** Coined by philosopher David Chalmers, the hard problem addresses why and how physical processes in the brain give rise to subjective experiences. This problem complicates the quest for machine consciousness, as it raises questions about whether machines can ever experience qualia—the subjective qualities of experiences.

- **Ethical Implications:** The potential for conscious machines raises ethical considerations regarding their treatment and rights. If a machine were to achieve consciousness, society would need to grapple with the moral implications of its existence and the responsibilities that come with it.

Conclusion

Theories and experiments in machine consciousness continue to evolve as researchers strive to understand the nature of consciousness itself. While significant progress has been made, the road ahead is filled with philosophical inquiries and ethical dilemmas. The implications of creating conscious machines could redefine our understanding of intelligence, existence, and what it means to be truly aware. As we venture further into this uncharted territory, the questions surrounding machine consciousness will only become more profound and urgent.

Implications for Humanity

The quest for strong artificial intelligence (AI) raises profound implications for humanity, challenging our understanding of consciousness, identity, and the very nature of existence. As we strive to create machines that can not only mimic human intelligence but also possess a form of consciousness, we must grapple with several critical questions: What does it mean to be human? Can machines possess emotions, creativity, or moral agency? And how will our relationship with technology evolve as we integrate intelligent systems into our daily lives?

The Nature of Consciousness

At the core of Kurzweil's vision for strong AI lies the question of consciousness. Traditional definitions of consciousness often revolve around self-awareness, perception, and the ability to experience emotions. However, the challenge of defining consciousness becomes evident when considering the possibility of machine consciousness. Can a computer, built from silicon and code, ever truly experience consciousness in the same way a human does?

Theories such as David Chalmers' "hard problem of consciousness" highlight the difficulty of explaining subjective experiences, or qualia, in purely physical terms. If we were to create a conscious machine, would it experience qualia in a manner analogous to humans, or would its existence be fundamentally different? This question becomes increasingly relevant as we develop AI systems that can simulate human-like interactions, raising ethical considerations regarding their treatment and rights.

Moral and Ethical Considerations

As AI systems approach human-like capabilities, the ethical implications of their existence must be addressed. If machines can think, feel, and make decisions, should they be granted rights similar to those of humans? This debate is compounded by the potential for AI to surpass human intelligence, leading to scenarios where machines could make choices that impact human lives.

The philosopher Nick Bostrom warns of the "control problem," where superintelligent AI could act in ways that are misaligned with human values. This raises the question: how do we ensure that the values embedded within AI systems reflect our ethical standards? The development of AI governance frameworks becomes crucial to mitigate risks associated with autonomous decision-making.

Economic and Social Impact

The rise of strong AI also presents significant economic implications. As machines become capable of performing tasks traditionally reserved for humans, the job market is likely to undergo a seismic shift. Industries reliant on routine cognitive tasks may face disruption, leading to widespread unemployment and economic inequality.

Kurzweil's predictions suggest that while some jobs will be lost, new roles will emerge in fields that require human creativity, empathy, and complex problem-solving. However, the transition may not be seamless. Workers displaced by AI may struggle to adapt, necessitating a robust educational framework to equip them with the skills needed for the future job market.

Human-AI Collaboration

Despite the potential challenges, the integration of strong AI into society can also lead to unprecedented opportunities for collaboration. As machines take on more complex tasks, humans can focus on areas where they excel—such as creativity, emotional intelligence, and interpersonal communication.

Kurzweil envisions a future where humans and machines work together synergistically, enhancing productivity and innovation. For instance, AI systems could analyze vast datasets to identify patterns, while humans interpret and apply these insights in creative and meaningful ways. This collaboration could lead to breakthroughs in fields such as medicine, environmental science, and education.

The Future of Human Identity

As we advance toward a future where strong AI becomes a reality, the implications for human identity cannot be overlooked. The merging of human and machine capabilities raises philosophical questions about what it means to be human. If we can augment our intelligence and cognitive abilities through technology, do we risk losing our essence as human beings?

Kurzweil's concept of the "singularity" suggests that the boundaries between human and machine will blur, leading to a new era of existence. This prospect invites a re-examination of our values, beliefs, and the very fabric of society. As we navigate this uncharted territory, it is imperative that we engage in thoughtful discourse about the implications of strong AI on our collective future.

Conclusion

In conclusion, the implications of strong AI for humanity are vast and multifaceted. As we stand on the brink of a technological revolution, it is essential to approach the development of AI with caution and foresight. By addressing the ethical, social, and philosophical challenges posed by strong AI, we can strive to create a future where humans and machines coexist harmoniously, enhancing our understanding of consciousness and expanding the horizons of human potential.

The New Mind

Brain-Machine Interfaces and Neural Implants

Brain-Machine Interfaces (BMIs), also known as Brain-Computer Interfaces (BCIs), represent a revolutionary frontier in the interplay between human cognition and technology. These systems create a direct communication pathway between the brain and external devices, enabling individuals to control machines using their neural activity. This section delves into the principles underlying BMIs, the various types of neural implants, their applications, challenges, and the ethical implications that accompany their development.

Theoretical Foundations of BMIs

At the core of BMIs is the understanding of how neural signals can be interpreted and translated into actionable commands. The brain communicates through electrical impulses generated by neurons, which can be captured using various techniques. The fundamental model of neuron communication can be described by the following equation:

$$I = g(V - V_{rev}) \tag{76}$$

where I is the current flowing through the neuron, g is the conductance, V is the membrane potential, and V_{rev} is the reversal potential. Understanding these dynamics is crucial for developing effective interfaces that can decode neural signals into commands for machines.

The primary methodologies for capturing neural activity include:

- **Invasive Techniques:** Such as implanted electrodes that directly interface with brain tissue, providing high-resolution data but carrying risks of surgical complications and long-term biocompatibility issues.

- **Non-invasive Techniques:** Such as electroencephalography (EEG), which measures electrical activity through the scalp. While safer, these methods often yield lower resolution and signal quality.

Types of Neural Implants

Neural implants can be categorized based on their functionality and the invasiveness of the procedure required to install them:

- **Cortical Implants:** These devices are placed directly on the surface of the brain. They have been used in research settings to allow paralyzed individuals to control robotic limbs or computer cursors through thought alone. A notable example is the BrainGate project, which has demonstrated the potential of cortical implants in restoring movement.

- **Deep Brain Stimulation (DBS):** This technique involves implanting electrodes in specific brain regions to modulate neural activity. It has been used successfully to treat conditions such as Parkinson's disease, providing symptomatic relief by altering the abnormal electrical patterns in the brain.

- **Peripheral Nerve Interfaces:** These interfaces connect to peripheral nerves rather than directly to the brain. They can be used to restore sensation or control prosthetic limbs, providing feedback to the user.

Applications of BMIs

The applications of BMIs and neural implants are vast and continue to evolve. They include:

- **Restoration of Movement:** BMIs have enabled paralyzed individuals to control robotic arms or cursors on a screen using only their thoughts. Studies have shown that with training, users can achieve remarkable control over these devices, demonstrating the potential for independence and improved quality of life.

- **Communication Aids:** For individuals with severe speech and motor impairments, BMIs can facilitate communication by allowing users to select words or phrases using their brain activity. This application is particularly poignant for those with conditions such as amyotrophic lateral sclerosis (ALS).

- **Cognitive Enhancement:** Research is ongoing into using BMIs for enhancing cognitive functions, such as memory and learning. Neural implants may provide stimulation to specific brain regions to improve memory retention or accelerate learning processes.

Challenges in Development and Implementation

Despite the promising potential of BMIs, several challenges remain:

- **Biocompatibility:** The long-term integration of implants with neural tissue poses significant challenges. The body's immune response can lead to inflammation and scarring, which may degrade the performance of the device over time.

- **Signal Decoding:** Accurately interpreting the complex patterns of neural activity is a daunting task. Advances in machine learning and signal processing are crucial for improving the accuracy and efficiency of decoding algorithms.

- **Ethical Concerns:** The enhancement of human capabilities through BMIs raises profound ethical questions. Issues surrounding consent, privacy, and the potential for misuse of technology must be carefully navigated as these technologies advance.

Ethical Implications of Neural Implants

The integration of technology with the human brain introduces ethical dilemmas that society must address. Some of the primary concerns include:

- **Identity and Agency:** As individuals augment their cognitive abilities or control devices with their thoughts, questions arise about the nature of identity and personal agency. Are these enhanced individuals still the same person, or does the technology alter their sense of self?

- **Access and Inequality:** The potential for cognitive enhancement through BMIs raises concerns about access to these technologies. If only a subset of the population can afford such enhancements, it could exacerbate existing inequalities.

- **Privacy Issues:** With devices capable of reading brain activity, the potential for unauthorized access to thoughts and intentions becomes a significant concern. Safeguarding personal mental data is paramount in the ethical deployment of BMIs.

Conclusion

The development of Brain-Machine Interfaces and neural implants holds transformative potential for medicine, communication, and human capability. As we stand on the brink of a new era in human-technology interaction, it is imperative to balance innovation with ethical considerations, ensuring that these advancements serve to enhance human life rather than complicate it. Raymond Kurzweil's vision of merging man and machine is not merely a futuristic concept but a burgeoning reality that demands our attention and thoughtful engagement.

The Future of Human Intelligence Augmentation

The future of human intelligence augmentation stands at the intersection of technology, neuroscience, and philosophy. As we delve into this complex terrain, we must consider the implications of enhancing human cognitive abilities through various means, including brain-machine interfaces (BMIs), neuropharmaceuticals, and genetic modifications.

Understanding Intelligence Augmentation

Intelligence augmentation (IA) refers to the enhancement of cognitive functions through technological means. The primary goal of IA is to improve human mental capabilities, enabling individuals to process information more efficiently, solve problems more creatively, and make better decisions. This concept can be mathematically represented through the augmentation function:

$$IA = f(C, T, E) \tag{77}$$

where IA is the level of intelligence augmentation, C represents cognitive capabilities, T denotes technological interventions, and E signifies environmental factors that influence learning and cognition.

Brain-Machine Interfaces

One of the most promising avenues for intelligence augmentation lies in the development of brain-machine interfaces (BMIs). BMIs facilitate direct communication between the brain and external devices, allowing for the transfer of information and control of technology through neural signals. For example, the work of companies like Neuralink demonstrates the potential of implantable devices that can decode brain activity and translate it into commands for computers or robotic limbs.

The mathematical modeling of BMI efficacy can be approached through signal processing algorithms, which analyze and interpret neural data. The relationship between neural signal fidelity and BMI performance can be expressed as:

$$P_{BMI} = \frac{SNR}{N} \tag{78}$$

where P_{BMI} is the performance of the BMI, SNR is the signal-to-noise ratio of the neural signals, and N represents the noise level in the system. Improving SNR through advanced materials and signal processing techniques is crucial for enhancing the effectiveness of BMIs.

Neuropharmaceuticals and Cognitive Enhancement

In parallel with BMIs, neuropharmaceuticals are emerging as a means to enhance cognitive functions. Substances such as nootropics, which are designed to improve memory, creativity, and motivation, are gaining popularity. Research into the effects of these compounds on brain chemistry reveals potential pathways for augmentation.

The relationship between neurotransmitter levels and cognitive performance can be modeled using the following equation:

$$C = k \cdot \left(\frac{NT}{T_{opt}}\right) \tag{79}$$

where C is cognitive performance, NT represents the concentration of neurotransmitters, T_{opt} is the optimal concentration for peak performance, and k is a constant that reflects individual variability. This model underscores the delicate balance required to achieve cognitive enhancement without adverse effects.

Ethical and Philosophical Considerations

While the prospects of intelligence augmentation are exciting, they also raise significant ethical and philosophical questions. The potential for unequal access to augmentation technologies could exacerbate existing societal inequalities. Moreover, the concept of what it means to be human may shift as cognitive enhancements blur the lines between natural and artificial intelligence.

For instance, if we consider the implications of augmenting intelligence through genetic modifications, we must address the ethical dilemmas surrounding designer babies and the potential loss of diversity in human cognition. The philosophical debate centers on whether enhanced individuals would retain their humanity or become something fundamentally different.

Challenges Ahead

Despite the promising advancements, several challenges remain in the field of intelligence augmentation. These include:

- **Technical Limitations:** Current BMIs are still in their infancy, with issues related to invasiveness, long-term stability, and data interpretation needing to be resolved.

- **Safety and Side Effects:** Neuropharmaceuticals may lead to unforeseen side effects, raising concerns about their long-term use and impact on mental health.

- **Regulatory Frameworks:** Establishing clear regulations around the development and use of augmentation technologies is essential to ensure safety and ethical standards.

- **Public Perception:** Societal acceptance of cognitive enhancements will play a critical role in their integration into everyday life. Education and dialogue will be vital in shaping public opinion.

THE NEW MIND

Conclusion

The future of human intelligence augmentation promises to reshape our understanding of cognition and the human experience. As we navigate this uncharted territory, it is imperative to balance innovation with ethical considerations, ensuring that the pursuit of enhanced intelligence serves the greater good. By fostering a collaborative dialogue between technologists, ethicists, and the public, we can harness the potential of intelligence augmentation while safeguarding our humanity.

Challenges and Ethical Considerations

The intersection of brain-machine interfaces (BMIs) and neural implants presents a myriad of challenges and ethical considerations that demand careful scrutiny. As we stand on the precipice of a new era of human augmentation, we must grapple with the implications of enhancing human capabilities through technology. This section explores the multifaceted issues surrounding these advancements, highlighting relevant theories, potential problems, and real-world examples.

Theoretical Foundations

The theoretical underpinning of BMIs is rooted in neuroengineering, a discipline that combines neuroscience and engineering to develop devices that can interact with the nervous system. One of the foundational theories is the **Neural Code Hypothesis**, which posits that information in the brain is represented by the patterns of neural activity. If we can decode these patterns, we can potentially translate thoughts into actionable commands for machines. The equation governing this relationship can be expressed as:

$$I(t) = \sum_{i=1}^{n} w_i \cdot a_i(t) \tag{80}$$

where $I(t)$ represents the output information at time t, w_i are the weights of the synaptic connections, and $a_i(t)$ is the activity of the ith neuron at time t.

This theoretical framework, while promising, raises significant ethical questions. For instance, if we can decode thoughts, who owns that information? Moreover, the potential for misuse of such technology looms large, as does the question of consent.

Potential Problems

The implementation of BMIs and neural implants introduces several potential problems, including:

- **Privacy Concerns:** As BMIs become more sophisticated, the risk of unauthorized access to an individual's thoughts and intentions increases. The concept of *mind reading* through technological means could lead to unprecedented invasions of privacy.

- **Inequality in Access:** The development of such technologies may exacerbate existing social inequalities. If only a select few can afford neural enhancements, a new class divide could emerge, where the augmented elite gain advantages over the non-augmented.

- **Identity and Autonomy:** The integration of technology into the human brain raises questions about personal identity and autonomy. As individuals enhance their cognitive abilities, the line between human and machine blurs, leading to existential dilemmas about what it means to be human.

- **Dependency on Technology:** With increased reliance on BMIs, there is a risk of diminishing natural cognitive abilities. If individuals become too dependent on technology for memory, learning, or decision-making, it could lead to a decline in critical thinking skills.

Real-World Examples

Several real-world examples illustrate the challenges and ethical considerations surrounding BMIs:

- **Neuralink:** Elon Musk's company Neuralink aims to develop implantable brain chips that could enable direct communication between humans and computers. While the potential benefits are immense, concerns have been raised about the ethical implications of such technology, particularly regarding informed consent and the possibility of coercion in its adoption.

- **Deep Brain Stimulation (DBS):** Used primarily to treat conditions like Parkinson's disease, DBS involves implanting electrodes in the brain to regulate abnormal impulses. While it has proven effective, ethical questions arise regarding the manipulation of mood and personality, as patients may experience changes in their sense of self.

- **Cyborg Anthropology:** This emerging field studies the interaction between humans and technology, raising questions about the societal implications of human augmentation. Researchers in this field emphasize the need for ethical frameworks to guide the development and implementation of BMIs.

Ethical Frameworks

To navigate the ethical landscape of BMIs and neural implants, several frameworks can be applied:

- **Utilitarianism:** This approach evaluates the ethicality of actions based on their outcomes. In the context of BMIs, a utilitarian perspective would weigh the potential benefits against the risks and harms to individuals and society.

- **Deontological Ethics:** This framework emphasizes the morality of actions themselves rather than their consequences. From a deontological standpoint, the act of implanting devices in human brains raises inherent ethical questions about consent, autonomy, and the sanctity of the human body.

- **Virtue Ethics:** Focusing on the character and virtues of individuals, this approach encourages the development of ethical technologists who prioritize humanity's well-being in their innovations.

Conclusion

As we venture further into the realm of brain-machine interfaces and neural implants, it is imperative that we address the challenges and ethical considerations that accompany these technologies. By fostering an open dialogue among technologists, ethicists, and the public, we can strive to ensure that the advancements in human augmentation enhance rather than diminish our humanity. The future of BMIs holds great promise, but it is our responsibility to navigate this landscape with caution, foresight, and a commitment to ethical principles.

Music, Art, and Creativity

Composing Music with AI

The intersection of artificial intelligence and music composition presents a fascinating landscape where creativity meets computation. This section explores the theoretical underpinnings, challenges, and notable examples of AI-driven music composition, highlighting how algorithms can mimic and innovate upon human creativity.

Theoretical Foundations

At the core of AI music composition lies a combination of machine learning algorithms and music theory. One of the most significant techniques employed is *neural networks*, particularly *recurrent neural networks* (RNNs) and their variant, *long short-term memory networks* (LSTMs). These architectures are adept at processing sequential data, making them ideal for handling the temporal nature of music.

The mathematical representation of a musical piece can be formalized as a sequence of notes, each characterized by various attributes such as pitch, duration, and intensity. If we denote a musical sequence as $S = (s_1, s_2, \ldots, s_n)$, where s_i represents the i-th note, the goal of an AI model is to learn the probability distribution of the next note given the previous notes:

$$P(s_i | s_1, s_2, \ldots, s_{i-1})$$

This can be achieved through training a neural network on a dataset of existing compositions, enabling the model to understand patterns and structures inherent in music.

Challenges in AI Music Composition

Despite advancements, AI music composition faces several challenges:

1. **Creativity vs. Imitation**: One of the primary criticisms of AI-generated music is its tendency to mimic existing styles rather than create original works. The balance between learning from past compositions and generating novel ideas is a delicate one.

2. **Emotional Depth**: Music is often a reflection of human emotions and experiences. While AI can analyze and replicate patterns, it struggles to infuse genuine emotional depth into compositions. This raises questions about the essence of creativity and whether machines can truly understand or convey emotion.

3. **Complexity of Music Theory**: Music is governed by intricate theoretical principles that dictate harmony, rhythm, and structure. Encoding these principles into algorithms remains a complex task, and deviations from established norms can lead to compositions that feel disjointed or unpleasing.

MUSIC, ART, AND CREATIVITY

4. **Evaluation Metrics**: Assessing the quality of AI-generated music poses a significant challenge. Traditional metrics used in music theory may not suffice, as subjective human responses play a crucial role in determining the appeal of a piece.

Notable Examples of AI in Music Composition

Several projects illustrate the potential of AI in music composition, showcasing both successes and ongoing challenges:

- **AIVA (Artificial Intelligence Virtual Artist)**: AIVA is an AI composer designed to create soundtracks for films, advertisements, and video games. By analyzing a vast dataset of classical music, AIVA generates compositions that evoke specific moods and styles, demonstrating a remarkable ability to mimic the works of human composers.

- **OpenAI's MuseNet**: MuseNet is an AI model capable of generating music in various styles, from classical to pop. It employs a deep learning architecture to predict subsequent notes in a composition, allowing it to blend different genres seamlessly. An example of its capability is the creation of a piece that combines elements of Bach with contemporary pop music.

- **Google's Magenta**: Magenta focuses on exploring the role of machine learning in the creative process. Through tools like *MusicVAE*, it enables users to create and manipulate melodies, showcasing how AI can assist human creativity rather than replace it. Users can input a melody, and the system generates variations, allowing for collaborative composition.

- **Jukedeck**: Jukedeck was a pioneer in AI-generated music for video content. It allowed users to customize parameters such as mood and tempo, generating unique tracks tailored to specific needs. Although Jukedeck has since shifted focus, it laid the groundwork for future AI music platforms.

Conclusion

The journey of composing music with AI is a testament to the evolving relationship between technology and creativity. While challenges remain, the potential for AI to augment human musical expression is immense. As algorithms become more sophisticated, the line between human and machine-generated music continues to blur, inviting us to reconsider our definitions of artistry and innovation. The future of music composition may not be solely about the notes played, but rather about the collaboration between human intuition and machine learning—a symphony of creativity that transcends traditional boundaries.

Bibliography

[1] AIVA. (2021). *Artificial Intelligence Virtual Artist*. Retrieved from `https://www.aiva.ai`

[2] OpenAI. (2019). *MuseNet: Generating Music with Deep Learning*. Retrieved from `https://openai.com/research/musenet`

[3] Google Brain Team. (2016). *Magenta: Music and Art Generation with Machine Learning*. Retrieved from `https://magenta.tensorflow.org`

[4] Jukedeck. (2018). *AI-Generated Music for Videos*. Retrieved from `https://www.jukedeck.com`

The Intersection of Machine Learning and Art

In recent years, the convergence of machine learning and art has sparked a revolution in how we understand creativity, expression, and the role of technology in artistic endeavors. This intersection is not merely a technological novelty; it raises profound questions about authorship, originality, and the very essence of art itself.

Theoretical Foundations

At the core of this intersection lies the concept of algorithmic creativity. This theory posits that machines can be programmed to produce creative works by mimicking human cognitive processes. One of the foundational models in this area is the Generative Adversarial Network (GAN), introduced by Ian Goodfellow in 2014. A GAN consists of two neural networks, the generator and the discriminator, that compete against each other in a zero-sum game. The generator creates images, while the discriminator evaluates them, providing feedback that enables the generator to improve its outputs.

The objective function for a GAN can be expressed as:

$$\min_{G} \max_{D} V(D, G) = \mathbb{E}_{x \sim p_{data}(x)}[\log D(x)] + \mathbb{E}_{z \sim p_z(z)}[\log(1 - D(G(z)))], \tag{81}$$

where G is the generator, D is the discriminator, $p_{data}(x)$ is the distribution of real data, and $p_z(z)$ is the distribution of the noise input to the generator.

This adversarial process leads to the generation of highly realistic images, music, and even literature, blurring the lines between human and machine creativity.

Examples of Machine Learning in Art

Several notable projects exemplify the integration of machine learning in the arts:

- **DeepArt:** Utilizing deep neural networks, DeepArt transforms photographs into artworks inspired by famous painters. By applying style transfer techniques, the algorithm can recreate the texture and color palette of artists like Van Gogh or Picasso.

- **AICAN:** Developed by Dr. Ahmed Elgammal and his team at Rutgers University, AICAN is an AI artist that creates original paintings. It has been trained on a dataset of over 80,000 artworks, allowing it to generate pieces that are often indistinguishable from those created by human artists. AICAN's work has been exhibited in galleries, prompting discussions on authorship and the role of the artist.

- **OpenAI's MuseNet:** This model can generate music in various styles, from classical to contemporary pop. By analyzing a vast dataset of compositions, MuseNet can create original pieces that reflect the nuances of different genres, showcasing the potential for AI to contribute to musical creativity.

Challenges and Ethical Considerations

Despite the exciting possibilities, the intersection of machine learning and art is fraught with challenges. One of the foremost concerns is the issue of originality. If a machine generates a piece of art, who owns the copyright? The creator of the algorithm? The user who inputs the data? Or the machine itself? This question remains largely unresolved and poses significant implications for intellectual property laws.

Additionally, there are ethical considerations regarding the potential for AI to perpetuate biases present in the training data. If an AI is trained on a dataset that lacks diversity, the art it produces may reflect those biases, leading to a homogenization of artistic expression. This raises questions about the inclusivity of AI-generated art and the responsibility of developers to ensure diverse representation.

The Future of Machine Learning in Art

Looking ahead, the integration of machine learning and art is likely to deepen. As algorithms become more sophisticated, they may not only assist artists but also collaborate with them. This collaborative approach can lead to new forms of art that challenge traditional notions of creativity.

Furthermore, the democratization of art production through accessible AI tools could empower a new generation of creators. Individuals without formal training can leverage machine learning to explore their artistic visions, fostering a more inclusive artistic landscape.

In conclusion, the intersection of machine learning and art is a dynamic and evolving field that challenges our understanding of creativity and originality. As technology continues to advance, it will be essential to navigate the ethical implications and embrace the potential for collaboration between humans and machines, ultimately enriching the tapestry of artistic expression.

Kurzweil's Contributions to the Field of Creativity

Raymond Kurzweil's influence extends far beyond the realms of artificial intelligence and technology; it reaches into the very heart of creativity itself. His innovative approaches have opened new avenues for artistic expression, fundamentally altering how we perceive the interplay between machines and human creativity.

The Intersection of Technology and Art

Kurzweil's journey into the world of creativity began with his pioneering work in music technology. In the 1980s, he developed the Kurzweil K250, one of the first digital synthesizers capable of accurately reproducing the sounds of traditional instruments. This groundbreaking device utilized a technique known as *sample-based synthesis*, which involves recording real instrument sounds and then manipulating them electronically. The K250 allowed musicians to create complex compositions with a rich palette of sounds, effectively democratizing music production.

$$f(t) = \sum_{n=1}^{N} a_n \cdot \sin(2\pi f_n t + \phi_n) \qquad (82)$$

where $f(t)$ represents the synthesized sound, a_n are the amplitudes, f_n are the frequencies of the harmonics, and ϕ_n are the phase shifts.

AI and Music Composition

Kurzweil's contributions to the field of creativity are not limited to musical instruments; they extend into the realm of artificial intelligence itself. He developed algorithms that enable machines to compose music autonomously. One notable example is the use of neural networks to analyze vast databases of musical compositions, learning patterns, styles, and structures. This approach allows AI to generate original pieces that can mimic the styles of legendary composers or create entirely new genres.

The algorithm can be represented as:

$$Y = f(X; \theta) \qquad (83)$$

where Y is the output music composition, X represents the input features (such as melodies, rhythms, and harmonies), and θ are the parameters of the neural network that are adjusted during training.

The Role of Creativity in AI

Kurzweil posits that creativity is not an exclusively human trait. He argues that machines can exhibit creative behaviors, challenging the traditional boundaries of what it means to be creative. This perspective is grounded in his belief that creativity arises from the ability to recognize patterns and make connections between disparate ideas. As AI systems become increasingly sophisticated, they can analyze and synthesize information in ways that parallel human thought processes.

Theoretical Frameworks

Kurzweil's exploration of creativity can be framed within several theoretical constructs. One such framework is the *Creativity Theory*, which suggests that creativity involves the synthesis of existing knowledge to produce novel ideas. This theory can be mathematically represented by the following relationship:

$$C = f(K, I) \qquad (84)$$

where C represents creativity, K is the existing knowledge base, and I denotes the individual's or machine's ability to integrate and innovate from that knowledge.

Challenges and Controversies

Despite Kurzweil's optimistic vision for AI and creativity, there are challenges and controversies surrounding the role of machines in creative fields. Critics argue that while AI can produce aesthetically pleasing works, it lacks the emotional depth and intentionality that characterize human creativity. The debate often centers around the question of whether a machine can truly understand the human experience or if it merely mimics human creativity without genuine insight.

Examples of AI in Creative Fields

Kurzweil's influence is evident in various projects that showcase AI's creative potential. One notable example is the collaboration between AI and human musicians, where algorithms generate compositions that are then refined by human artists. This collaborative approach has led to innovative musical genres, blending traditional techniques with modern technology.

Another example is the use of AI in visual arts, where algorithms analyze existing artworks to generate new pieces. Programs such as *DeepArt* and *Artbreeder* allow users to create original images by merging styles and elements from various sources, demonstrating the potential for AI to contribute to visual creativity.

Conclusion

Raymond Kurzweil's contributions to the field of creativity illustrate the profound impact of technology on artistic expression. His work challenges us to reconsider the boundaries of creativity and the role of machines in the creative process. As we continue to explore the intersection of AI and art, we may find that the future of creativity is not solely human but a collaborative endeavor between man and machine. This fusion has the potential to unlock new forms of expression and redefine what it means to be creative in an increasingly digital world.

The Legacy Continues

The Next Generation of Innovators

As we stand on the precipice of a new technological era, the legacy of Raymond Kurzweil is not merely a historical artifact but a living, breathing force that continues to inspire and shape the minds of the next generation of innovators. These young visionaries, equipped with the knowledge and tools developed by pioneers like Kurzweil, are poised to tackle the challenges of the future, pushing the boundaries of artificial intelligence, machine learning, and human-computer interaction.

Empowering Young Innovators

Kurzweil's influence can be seen in the rising tide of educational programs and initiatives aimed at fostering innovation among youth. Organizations such as *Code.org* and *Girls Who Code* are instrumental in providing resources and learning opportunities for students of all backgrounds, encouraging them to engage with technology at an early age. These programs emphasize the importance of computational thinking, creativity, and problem-solving skills, essential traits for the innovators of tomorrow.

The Role of AI in Education

In the realm of education, Kurzweil's predictions about personalized learning are coming to fruition. Adaptive learning technologies, powered by artificial intelligence, are revolutionizing the classroom experience. For instance, platforms like *Knewton* and *DreamBox* use algorithms to tailor educational content to individual student needs, allowing for a more customized learning experience. This shift not only enhances student engagement but also prepares them for a future where adaptability and lifelong learning are paramount.

Challenges Faced by Young Innovators

However, the journey of the next generation is not without its hurdles. As they navigate a rapidly changing technological landscape, they must confront significant challenges, including ethical dilemmas surrounding AI, privacy concerns, and the societal impact of automation. The question of *"Who benefits from AI?"* looms large, as the potential for job displacement and economic inequality becomes increasingly apparent.

To address these challenges, young innovators must be equipped with a robust ethical framework. This includes understanding the implications of their work and striving to create technology that serves humanity as a whole. As Kurzweil himself has stated, "The key to the future of humanity is in the hands of the next generation of innovators."

Examples of Emerging Innovators

Several young innovators exemplify the spirit of Kurzweil's legacy. For instance, *Tanmay Bakshi*, a prodigious coder and AI enthusiast, began programming at the age of five and has since developed applications that utilize machine learning for social good. His work on AI-powered chatbots demonstrates how technology can enhance communication and accessibility, echoing Kurzweil's vision of using technology to improve human life.

Another notable figure is *Gitanjali Rao*, a 15-year-old inventor recognized as *TIME* magazine's Kid of the Year in 2020. Rao has developed devices to detect lead in drinking water and has created a unique app to combat cyberbullying. Her work not only showcases the innovative spirit of her generation but also emphasizes the importance of addressing pressing global issues through technology.

The Future of Innovation

Looking ahead, the potential for the next generation of innovators is boundless. As Kurzweil posits in his theory of the *Singularity*, the fusion of human intelligence and artificial intelligence could lead to unprecedented advancements in various fields, from healthcare to environmental sustainability. The equation governing this exponential growth can be expressed as:

$$I(t) = I_0 \cdot e^{rt} \tag{85}$$

where $I(t)$ represents the level of innovation at time t, I_0 is the initial level of innovation, r is the growth rate, and e is the base of the natural logarithm. This equation illustrates how innovation compounds over time, suggesting that the innovations of today will pave the way for even greater breakthroughs tomorrow.

As young innovators harness the power of AI and other emerging technologies, they will undoubtedly face challenges and ethical questions. However, with a solid foundation built on the principles established by Kurzweil and a commitment to using technology for the greater good, they will be well-equipped to lead us into a future that is not only technologically advanced but also socially responsible.

In conclusion, the next generation of innovators stands on the shoulders of giants like Raymond Kurzweil. With an eye toward the future and a heart dedicated to improving the human experience, they are ready to tackle the challenges ahead, ensuring that the legacy of innovation and inspiration continues to thrive in an ever-evolving world.

Kurzweil's Influence on Future Technological Developments

Raymond Kurzweil's visionary insights have shaped the trajectory of technological advancements in profound ways. His predictions and innovations have not only influenced the fields of artificial intelligence and machine learning but have also set the stage for future developments that could redefine human existence. This section explores the multifaceted impact of Kurzweil's ideas on upcoming technological trends, emphasizing the interplay between innovation, ethical considerations, and societal implications.

The Exponential Growth of Technology

At the heart of Kurzweil's philosophy is the concept of exponential growth in technology, encapsulated in his law of accelerating returns. This theory posits that the rate of technological progress is not linear but exponential, leading to rapid advancements that can transform entire industries. Mathematically, this can be represented as:

$$T(n) = T(n-1) + k \cdot T(n-1) \quad \text{where } k > 1 \tag{86}$$

where $T(n)$ is the technological capability at iteration n, and k is a constant representing the growth factor. This exponential growth has implications for various sectors, including healthcare, education, and communication, suggesting that the pace of innovation will continue to accelerate, leading to unforeseen breakthroughs.

Artificial Intelligence and Machine Learning

Kurzweil's contributions to artificial intelligence have laid the groundwork for future advancements in machine learning and neural networks. His work on natural language processing and speech recognition has catalyzed the development of more sophisticated AI systems capable of understanding and generating human language. For instance, the introduction of deep learning techniques has revolutionized AI applications, enabling machines to learn from vast datasets and improve their performance over time.

Consider the function representing the learning process of a neural network:

$$L(\theta) = \frac{1}{m} \sum_{i=1}^{m} (h_\theta(x^{(i)}) - y^{(i)})^2 \tag{87}$$

where L is the loss function, θ represents the parameters of the model, $h_\theta(x)$ is the hypothesis function, m is the number of training examples, and y is the actual output. Kurzweil's influence is evident in the way contemporary AI systems are designed to mimic human cognitive processes, pushing the boundaries of what machines can achieve.

Healthcare and Longevity

Kurzweil's quest for extending human life through technology has sparked a revolution in the healthcare sector. His predictions about the convergence of biotechnology, nanotechnology, and information technology have inspired researchers to explore innovative solutions for age-related diseases. The potential for gene editing technologies, such as CRISPR, to enhance human health and longevity exemplifies Kurzweil's vision.

The relationship between technological advancement and lifespan can be modeled as:

$$L = L_0 + \alpha \cdot e^{\beta t} \tag{88}$$

where L is the expected lifespan, L_0 is the baseline lifespan, α is a constant representing the impact of technology, β is the growth rate of technological advancement, and t is time. This equation illustrates how technological innovations could potentially increase human lifespan, aligning with Kurzweil's aspirations for a healthier future.

Education and Personalized Learning

The influence of Kurzweil extends into the realm of education, where his ideas about personalized learning and adaptive technologies are reshaping teaching methodologies. By leveraging AI and data analytics, educational institutions can tailor learning experiences to individual students, addressing their unique needs and learning styles.

The effectiveness of personalized learning can be assessed using the following function:

$$E = \sum_{i=1}^{n} w_i \cdot p_i \tag{89}$$

where E is the overall effectiveness of the educational program, w_i is the weight assigned to each learning method, and p_i represents the performance metrics of students. Kurzweil's vision encourages a shift from traditional one-size-fits-all approaches to more dynamic and responsive educational environments.

Ethical Implications and Challenges

While Kurzweil's influence on technological developments is significant, it also raises important ethical considerations. The rapid advancement of AI and biotechnology presents challenges related to privacy, security, and the moral implications of enhancing human capabilities. As we embrace these technologies, it is crucial to establish frameworks that address potential risks and ensure responsible innovation.

One critical area of concern is the impact of AI on employment. As machines become increasingly capable, the displacement of human workers poses a significant challenge. The relationship between automation and employment can be represented as:

$$J_t = J_0 \cdot e^{-\lambda t} \tag{90}$$

where J_t is the number of jobs at time t, J_0 is the initial number of jobs, and λ is the rate of job displacement due to automation. This equation highlights the need for proactive measures to prepare the workforce for a future where AI plays a dominant role.

Conclusion

In conclusion, Raymond Kurzweil's influence on future technological developments is far-reaching and multifaceted. His insights into the exponential growth of technology, advancements in artificial intelligence, and the quest for human longevity have set the stage for a future that promises both incredible opportunities and significant challenges. As we navigate this rapidly changing landscape, it is essential to embrace Kurzweil's vision while remaining vigilant about the ethical implications of our technological pursuits. By doing so, we can harness the power of innovation to create a better future for all.

The Power of a Singular Vision

Raymond Kurzweil's journey through the landscape of technology and artificial intelligence has been marked by a singular vision: the belief that technology can fundamentally enhance human capabilities and ultimately lead to a new era of existence. This vision, often seen as audacious, has driven Kurzweil to challenge the status quo and push the boundaries of what is possible.

At the heart of Kurzweil's philosophy is the concept of exponential growth in technology, famously articulated in his law of accelerating returns. This theory posits that the rate of technological progress is not linear but exponential. In mathematical terms, if we denote the progress of technology as $P(t)$, where t is time, Kurzweil's law can be expressed as:

$$P(t) = P_0 \cdot e^{kt}$$

where P_0 is the initial state of technology, k is a constant representing the rate of growth, and e is the base of the natural logarithm. This equation illustrates how technological advancements build upon each other, leading to rapid and often unforeseen developments.

Kurzweil's vision is not merely theoretical; it has practical implications across various domains. For instance, in the field of health and longevity, his work has inspired innovations in biotechnology that aim to extend human lifespan. By integrating biological and technological advancements, such as genetic engineering and nanotechnology, Kurzweil envisions a future where diseases are not only treated but prevented. This perspective is exemplified by his advocacy for personalized medicine, which tailors treatments based on an individual's genetic makeup.

However, the pursuit of such a vision is fraught with challenges and ethical dilemmas. One major concern is the potential for inequality in access to these advancements. As technology progresses, there is a risk that only a privileged few will benefit from life-extending technologies, leaving others behind. This disparity raises critical questions about the moral implications of human enhancement and the societal structures that govern access to such technologies.

Moreover, Kurzweil's predictions about the future of artificial intelligence have sparked intense debate. His assertion that machines will achieve human-level intelligence by the mid-21st century has been met with skepticism and concern. Critics argue that the pursuit of strong AI poses existential risks, including the potential for machines to surpass human control. The implications of such a scenario are profound, as they challenge our understanding of consciousness, agency, and what it means to be human.

Kurzweil addresses these concerns by emphasizing the importance of ethical frameworks in the development of AI. He advocates for a collaborative approach, where technologists, ethicists, and policymakers work together to ensure that AI is developed responsibly. This collaborative vision is crucial in navigating the complexities of a future where AI plays an integral role in society.

In the realm of creativity, Kurzweil's singular vision has also left an indelible mark. His work in music and art demonstrates how technology can augment human creativity rather than replace it. By employing algorithms that analyze and generate music, Kurzweil has shown that machines can serve as collaborators in the creative process. This intersection of technology and artistry not only expands the boundaries of what is possible but also redefines our understanding of creativity itself.

Ultimately, the power of a singular vision lies in its ability to inspire and mobilize. Kurzweil's unwavering belief in the potential of technology to enhance human existence has motivated countless innovators and thinkers to pursue their own visions. As we stand on the brink of unprecedented technological advancements, the challenge remains: how can we harness this power responsibly and ethically?

In conclusion, Raymond Kurzweil's legacy is a testament to the impact of a singular vision on the trajectory of technology and society. His theories and innovations have not only shaped the fields of artificial intelligence and biotechnology but have also sparked critical discussions about the future of humanity. As we navigate the complexities of this new era, Kurzweil's insights serve as a guiding light, encouraging us to embrace the possibilities while remaining vigilant about the ethical implications of our choices.

Index

2040s, 24

a, 1–5, 7–14, 16–27, 29, 31–33, 35,
    36, 38–41, 43, 46, 47,
    49–55, 58–60, 62, 65–72,
    75–77, 79–85, 87–90, 94,
    95, 100, 102, 104–107,
    111, 113, 115, 116,
    119–121, 123, 125–130
ability, 9, 10, 18, 20, 25, 29, 31, 33,
    44, 47, 49, 53, 54, 59, 76,
    86, 88, 92, 93, 105, 122
acceleration, 22
acceptance, 8, 33
access, 13, 18–21, 70, 84, 86, 92,
    112, 129
accessibility, 9, 12, 14, 19–21, 51,
    59, 68, 70
acclaim, 13
account, 16, 32, 33
accountability, 24, 26, 28, 32, 35, 38,
    50
accuracy, 13, 18, 20, 25, 39, 44, 62
achievement, 16
act, 50, 89, 106
activity, 44, 108
adaptability, 44
addition, 6, 12, 22

address, 18, 20, 29, 35, 38, 69, 71,
    80, 85, 110, 112, 115, 128
adherence, 34
adoption, 73, 76, 86
advance, 45, 68, 95, 107, 121
advancement, 22, 23, 25, 31, 127,
    128
advent, 19
adventure, 7
advocacy, 32, 129
advocate, 85
affection, 54
age, 1–4, 8, 10, 40, 75, 81, 84, 127
agency, 34, 50, 52, 129
aging, 79, 82, 83
AI, 101
Alan Turing, 46, 54
algorithm, 120, 122
alleviation, 24
allocation, 80, 82
ambiguity, 71, 94
analysis, 39, 75, 95
animation, 70
anonymization, 38
application, 3
approach, 3, 10, 14, 24, 26, 32, 33,
    52, 68, 71, 80, 85, 89, 96,
    106, 107, 121–123, 129

area, 11, 128
argument, 49
arithmetic, 6
art, 119–121, 123
Arthur C. Clarke, 2
artifact, 123
aspiration, 79
assertion, 32, 129
assistance, 50
attempt, 103
attention, 16, 52, 94
attribute, 46, 49
audio, 19
auditing, 34
augmentation, 111–113, 115
authenticity, 49, 50
authorship, 119
automation, 22, 26, 39, 128
autonomy, 21, 34, 38, 47, 50, 51, 53, 54
availability, 19
awareness, 14, 19, 49, 105
awe, 59

backbone, 5
background, 96
backpropagation, 67
balance, 39, 65, 113
bandwidth, 78
bank, 71
barrier, 19, 94
basic, 5, 72
beginning, 7, 68, 77
behavior, 6, 49, 50, 54
being, 24, 25, 31, 33, 34, 50, 87–89, 102
belief, 4, 7, 12, 65, 80, 122
benefit, 29, 52, 59, 129
bias, 22, 26, 28, 32, 34

biology, 79, 80, 83
biotechnology, 79, 127–130
bit, 5
blending, 123
blur, 22, 41, 50, 102, 107, 112
body, 76
brain, 32, 44, 102, 107, 110, 111, 115
brand, 95
breadth, 33
breakthrough, 12, 16
breathing, 123
bridge, 12, 19
brink, 25, 43, 50, 76, 80, 83, 102, 107
building, 7, 10, 21, 75, 88
business, 12, 40, 95

camp, 2
capability, 21, 25, 47
career, 3, 5, 7
case, 47, 54
catalyst, 14, 27
caution, 55, 107, 115
cease, 54
cell, 80
century, 85, 89, 129
challenge, 3, 4, 7, 13, 26, 31, 32, 35, 36, 44, 47, 50, 51, 68, 76, 93–95, 105, 121, 128, 129
change, 14, 24, 27, 41, 87
character, 13
chemistry, 111
childhood, 1, 3
Chomsky, 71
circuit, 5
city, 1
clarity, 16
class, 32, 51

Index 133

classroom, 18, 89
climate, 24
code, 105
coding, 10
coercion, 51
cognition, 31, 33, 49, 112, 113
collaboration, 9, 36, 75, 79, 86, 88, 89, 106, 121, 123
combination, 13, 58
command, 72
commitment, 12, 14, 17, 36, 53, 115, 125
communication, 46, 100, 108
community, 12, 13, 17, 18, 20, 21, 32, 58, 75
compassion, 14, 52
complexity, 93
compliance, 36
composition, 115–117
comprehension, 54
computation, 115
computer, 2, 4–7, 10, 32, 62, 105, 124
computing, 2, 5, 7, 21, 75
concept, 2, 4, 10, 22, 23, 31, 41, 46, 50, 51, 73, 75, 107, 112, 126
concern, 80, 128, 129
conclusion, 5, 14, 21, 23, 27, 29, 31, 33, 36, 40, 46, 48, 50, 53, 55, 65, 68, 70, 72, 75, 76, 79, 83, 85, 87, 91, 95, 100, 102, 107, 121, 125, 128, 130
conference, 16
confidence, 16
connection, 49
consciousness, 7, 31, 32, 46, 49–51, 54, 103–105, 107, 129

consent, 32, 47, 51, 113
consideration, 35, 50, 51
construct, 85
construction, 5
constructivism, 86
content, 86, 88
context, 51, 54, 62, 71, 86, 94
contract, 8
contrast, 34
contribution, 69
control, 22, 34, 44, 106, 129
controversy, 32
convention, 59
convergence, 119, 127
conversation, 46, 49, 55
copyright, 120
core, 12, 21, 34, 57, 60, 71, 85, 93, 105, 107
cornerstone, 13
cost, 26
creation, 7, 8, 12, 26, 35, 40
creativity, 7, 24, 26, 51, 52, 79, 106, 111, 115, 116, 119–123
creator, 120
culmination, 13
culture, 33, 38, 52
curiosity, 1–3, 5, 7, 8, 10, 12
current, 19, 22
curriculum, 86
curve, 4, 20
customer, 39, 95
cutting, 10

data, 5, 25, 26, 28, 34, 38, 39, 47, 52, 65, 72, 78, 86, 92, 94, 95, 111, 120, 127
dataset, 116, 120
David Chalmers', 105
day, 21

debate, 31, 106, 112, 123, 129
decision, 50, 54, 106
declaration, 7
dedication, 12
definition, 32
degradation, 44
degree, 11
dehumanization, 52
demand, 26, 39, 40
democratization, 121
deontology, 34
deployment, 26, 32, 35, 39
depth, 33, 51, 123
descent, 67
design, 4, 38
designer, 112
desire, 2, 3, 7, 8, 12
determination, 7, 14
developer, 50
development, 13, 17, 24, 26, 33, 35, 44, 49, 54, 58, 59, 65, 69, 70, 72, 80, 85, 87–89, 94, 96, 98, 106, 107, 126, 129
device, 8, 13, 20, 58, 69
diagnostic, 22
dialogue, 27, 29, 33, 36, 50, 85, 113, 115
difference, 12, 21
difficulty, 105
dignity, 38, 53
dilemma, 50
disabled, 16
discomfort, 76
disconnect, 76
discourse, 31, 48, 50, 53, 107
discussion, 46, 103
disease, 24
disorientation, 76
disparity, 84, 129

displacement, 26, 35, 128
disruption, 35, 106
distinction, 49
distribution, 14
divergence, 51
diversity, 94, 112, 121
divide, 19, 24, 32, 51, 80, 84, 86, 92
domain, 103
dream, 14, 80, 81, 83
drive, 1, 24
duty, 34
dynamic, 26, 41, 68, 90, 121

economic, 22, 26, 27, 29, 35, 106
economy, 24, 40
edge, 10
editing, 127
education, 9, 12, 19, 24, 26, 41, 68, 70, 76, 85–87, 89–92, 102, 106, 127
effectiveness, 89, 127
efficacy, 18, 111
efficiency, 26, 27, 47, 52, 59
electronic, 5, 8
Eliezer Yudkowsky, 51
Elon Musk's, 50
embodiment, 4
embrace, 8, 40, 50, 55, 121, 128, 130
emergence, 24, 75
emotion, 33, 70
empathy, 16, 52, 54, 106
emphasis, 32
employment, 9, 35, 40, 128
empowerment, 18
encounter, 2
end, 10
endeavor, 4, 8, 14, 43, 80, 102, 123
endorsement, 8
energy, 84

Index 135

engagement, 5, 19, 27, 50, 70, 75, 86, 88
engineering, 80, 129
enhance, 4, 7, 12, 14, 21, 24, 35, 41, 43, 44, 51, 52, 54, 55, 59, 70, 75, 79, 83, 85, 86, 88, 102, 111, 115, 127
enhancement, 32, 46, 51–53, 69, 90, 129
entertainment, 68, 70, 76
entity, 32
entrepreneurship, 8–10
environment, 3, 78, 85, 87
equality, 53
equation, 6, 13, 22, 26, 28, 34, 35, 39, 44, 69, 70, 86, 88, 89, 94, 108, 111
equity, 84, 87
era, 23, 25, 43, 50, 53, 76, 83, 102, 107, 123, 130
eradication, 24
erosion, 47
error, 34, 67
essence, 5, 9, 25, 43, 50, 107, 119
esteem, 76
evaluation, 28
event, 22
evidence, 25
evolution, 31, 40, 50, 60, 95
exacerbation, 32
examination, 23, 107
example, 20, 24, 26, 28, 31, 34, 54, 72, 94, 122, 123
excitement, 59
exercise, 5, 55
existence, 3, 25, 32, 83, 85, 105–107, 126
expectancy, 80, 84
expense, 49

experience, 2, 7, 12, 22, 51–53, 55, 70, 75, 76, 78, 82, 87, 88, 105, 113, 123, 125
experimentation, 89
exploitation, 54
exploration, 2, 5, 7, 41, 43, 55, 68, 102, 104
exposure, 10
expression, 119, 121, 123
expressiveness, 70
extension, 80, 85
extent, 22, 47, 54
eye, 125

fabric, 3, 31, 83, 107
face, 9, 22, 26, 84, 106, 125
faire, 32
fairness, 28, 34, 35, 51, 52
fantasy, 80
fascination, 3–5, 10, 41
father, 4
fear, 35
feasibility, 33
feat, 4
feedback, 4, 22, 95
fiction, 2
field, 4, 7, 10, 12, 19, 20, 32, 46, 58, 59, 64, 65, 68, 70, 72, 83, 95, 112, 121–123, 129
finding, 2
flexibility, 40
focus, 12, 32
following, 4, 5, 9, 13, 33–35, 39, 44, 75, 84, 86, 108, 111, 127
food, 84
foray, 7
force, 10, 14, 85, 123
forefront, 14, 81, 83
foresight, 23, 107, 115

form, 3, 32
format, 70
formula, 27
foster, 27, 29, 33, 52, 75, 79, 87, 88
foundation, 10, 12, 97, 125
founding, 14
fraction, 19
framework, 13, 32, 36, 71, 106, 113
freelance, 40
fulfillment, 85
function, 9, 34, 51, 119, 126, 127
functionality, 21, 108
fusion, 123
future, 1, 2, 7, 8, 10, 12, 14, 19, 22–25, 27, 29, 31–33, 36, 38, 39, 41, 43, 46–48, 50, 53, 55, 65, 68, 70, 75–77, 80, 89, 92, 100, 102, 106, 107, 113, 115, 123–126, 128–130
futurism, 23, 31, 33, 79, 81

game, 2
gap, 9, 12, 19, 93
gene, 127
generation, 14, 21, 90, 95, 120, 121, 124, 125
genetic, 32, 80, 112, 129
gig, 40
goal, 44, 57, 60, 81
good, 10, 14, 26, 33, 113, 125
governance, 106
government, 14
graduate, 11
grammar, 71
grasp, 80
groundbreaking, 5, 8, 10, 12, 13, 17, 20, 45, 46, 69, 97, 102

groundwork, 3, 5, 7, 10, 14, 59, 72, 126
growth, 4, 21, 23, 27, 31, 40, 75, 76, 80, 84, 89, 126, 128

handling, 96
happiness, 34
hardware, 4, 22, 58, 75
harm, 50
have, 12, 14, 17, 21, 31–34, 39, 51, 61, 62, 65, 67, 68, 70, 71, 76, 81, 92, 94, 95, 97, 104, 121, 126–130
head, 85
health, 76, 83, 84, 127, 129
healthcare, 22, 25–27, 68, 76, 127
heart, 41, 44, 68, 95, 103, 121, 125, 126
help, 18, 89
hobby, 5
homogenization, 121
hope, 20
household, 3
human, 2–5, 7, 11–13, 22–24, 26, 31–33, 38, 41, 43, 46, 48–55, 62, 65, 69–72, 75, 76, 79–83, 85, 93, 95, 100, 102, 105–107, 110, 112, 113, 115, 116, 120–129
humanity, 7, 10, 25, 31, 36, 43, 49, 50, 52, 53, 65, 77, 80, 81, 103, 107, 112, 113, 115, 130
hypothesis, 71

idea, 2
identity, 10, 32, 49–51, 76, 107
image, 57
imagination, 83

Index

immersion, 73, 75
immortality, 32, 33
impact, 9, 12, 13, 18, 20–22, 26, 27, 35, 38, 39, 50, 67, 70, 76, 80, 85, 97, 106, 123, 126, 128, 130
implant, 54
implementation, 28, 44, 114
importance, 9, 24, 28, 80, 86, 94, 129
inception, 60
inclusion, 18, 20
inclusivity, 21, 29, 121
income, 40, 86
increase, 21, 39, 75, 84
independence, 16, 18, 20
individual, 12, 32, 34, 38, 47, 50, 52, 54, 78, 85, 86, 88, 127, 129
individuality, 87
industry, 8, 70
inequality, 35, 106, 129
infancy, 10
influence, 10, 85, 121, 123, 127, 128
information, 5, 13, 17, 19–21, 34, 49, 59, 79, 113, 122, 127
ingenuity, 72, 83
innovation, 2, 7–10, 12, 14, 16, 17, 21, 23, 29, 60, 65, 89, 95, 106, 113, 125, 126, 128
input, 72
inquiry, 2, 88
insight, 123
inspiration, 2, 125
instance, 18–20, 22, 24, 25, 28, 32, 34, 39, 49–52, 54, 70–72, 76, 89, 106, 112, 113, 126, 129
institution, 71
instruction, 89

integration, 22, 23, 26, 28, 29, 31, 34, 41, 43, 47, 50, 54, 70, 75, 78, 79, 85, 88, 90, 110, 120, 121
intelligence, 1, 2, 4, 5, 7, 10, 12–14, 19, 22, 23, 26, 31–33, 41, 46, 50–54, 60, 65, 68, 72, 75, 78, 79, 81, 101–103, 105–107, 112, 113, 115, 121, 122, 124, 126, 128–130
intent, 7
intentionality, 49, 123
interaction, 3, 33, 46, 62, 70, 76, 79, 100, 124
interactivity, 73
interest, 1, 11
internet, 86
interplay, 4, 7, 23, 50, 77, 95, 121, 126
interpretation, 71, 94
intersection, 14, 19, 37, 46, 75, 79, 83, 100, 115, 119–121, 123
intonation, 69
introduction, 9, 18, 20, 126
invasiveness, 108
invention, 8, 13, 16
investment, 26
Isaac Asimov, 2
isolation, 49
issue, 69, 76, 86, 94, 120

Jean Piaget, 3
job, 22, 26, 27, 35, 39–41, 106
John Searle's, 49
journey, 1, 4, 5, 7, 8, 10, 12, 14, 17, 20, 27, 43, 62, 68, 72, 85, 89, 102

key, 5, 17, 31, 57, 60, 63, 69, 73, 94, 95, 104
knack, 8
knowledge, 3, 10, 83, 85, 87, 89, 90, 102, 124
Kurzweil, 21

labor, 26
lack, 19, 31, 33, 69, 86, 94
landscape, 12, 21, 29, 40, 41, 48, 50, 51, 62, 68, 85, 87, 89, 90, 115, 121, 128
language, 11, 13, 49, 60, 62, 68, 69, 71, 72, 93–95, 97, 98, 126
latency, 78
law, 23, 126
lead, 4, 7, 22, 32, 33, 47, 49, 51, 52, 75, 76, 84, 88, 106, 121, 125
learner, 85
learning, 3, 4, 10, 12–14, 18, 20, 27, 44, 57, 65–68, 70, 85–89, 92, 95, 97, 100, 119–122, 124, 126, 127
legacy, 14, 19, 21, 123, 125, 130
level, 19, 22, 23, 39, 80, 129
leverage, 86, 88, 121
life, 2, 5, 7, 14, 19, 29, 32, 34, 38, 44, 47, 52, 54, 70, 79–85, 102, 127, 129
lifespan, 81, 83, 127, 129
lifetime, 2, 12
light, 102, 130
lighting, 18
like, 2, 31, 32, 49, 51, 60, 62, 95, 105, 106, 124, 125
line, 50, 54
linguistic, 68
literature, 16, 19, 25, 120

living, 4, 123
longevity, 83–85, 127–129
loom, 28
loop, 22
loss, 112
love, 8, 89

machine, 2, 4, 5, 10, 12–14, 16, 18, 20, 22, 32, 41–44, 46, 49, 50, 54, 55, 57–59, 65, 67–71, 93, 95, 97, 100, 102–105, 107, 115, 119–121, 123, 124, 126
mainstream, 12, 20
makeup, 129
making, 14, 17, 54, 94, 106
man, 41–43, 94, 123
management, 25
manifestation, 12
manipulation, 5, 32, 50, 69
manner, 33, 36, 105
manufacturing, 39
market, 8, 9, 14, 22, 26, 27, 39–41, 106
marketing, 95
Martin Heidegger, 55
Massachusetts, 10
master, 11
material, 70
mean, 49, 51
meaning, 23, 85
means, 7, 10, 32, 43, 48, 50, 51, 81, 105, 107, 111, 112, 122, 123, 129
measure, 31
media, 33, 95
medicine, 22, 24, 102, 106, 129
memory, 111
mentor, 88

Index

mentoring, 89
mentorship, 10
merging, 32, 41–43, 107
method, 69
metric, 34
microchip, 21
microcosm, 7
milestone, 19, 23, 59, 62
million, 26
mind, 3, 41
mindset, 40
misidentification, 34
misinformation, 78
mission, 58
misuse, 24, 32, 47, 52, 54, 113
model, 3, 20, 68, 69, 84, 87, 94, 98, 108, 116
modeling, 70, 97, 111
moment, 2, 14
money, 8
monitoring, 28
Moore, 21, 24
mortality, 79, 80
motivation, 86, 111
movement, 21, 81
music, 8, 115–117, 120, 122
musician, 8

name, 23, 47
nanotechnology, 79, 127, 129
naturalness, 13, 69, 70
nature, 2, 7, 8, 20, 26, 40, 46, 51, 76, 82, 103, 105
nausea, 76
need, 13, 19, 26, 33, 34, 40, 89, 92
network, 66, 67, 116, 126
neuron, 66, 108
neuroplasticity, 44
neuroscience, 2, 46

neurotransmitter, 111
New York, 1
Nick Bostrom, 51, 106
Noam Chomsky, 71
noise, 44, 62, 96
non, 21
Norbert Wiener, 4
norm, 51
normalization, 52
not, 1–8, 10, 12, 14, 16–25, 29, 31–33, 36, 38, 43, 46, 48–50, 52, 54, 55, 64, 67, 68, 70, 79, 80, 83, 87, 88, 97, 102, 106, 119, 121–123, 125, 126, 129, 130
notion, 21, 33, 85, 86
novelty, 119
number, 2, 21

object, 72
objective, 119
observation, 4, 75
off, 8, 35
on, 2, 3, 5, 11–14, 16, 18–25, 28, 29, 31, 32, 34, 35, 39, 40, 43, 46, 49–52, 57, 60, 65, 70, 72, 76, 80, 83–86, 89, 92–95, 97, 102, 103, 106–108, 111, 112, 116, 120, 123, 125, 126, 128–130
one, 7, 12, 14, 36, 43, 103
operation, 6
opinion, 95
opportunity, 7
optimism, 33, 80
originality, 119–121
other, 9, 18, 21, 53, 125

outlook, 24, 83
output, 52, 66, 67
outset, 38
over, 34, 39, 52, 65, 92, 126
overpopulation, 80, 82, 84
oversight, 26
oversimplification, 33

paradigm, 41, 88, 89
parallel, 111, 122
part, 10
passion, 8, 10, 16
path, 102
patient, 25, 26
pattern, 11, 57
people, 2, 9, 75, 85
perception, 95, 105
performance, 18, 52, 65, 86, 88, 111, 126
period, 7, 10
perseverance, 8, 72
person, 14, 32, 54
persona, 33
personality, 54
personalization, 27
perspective, 34, 52, 75, 122, 129
phase, 13
phenomenon, 23, 33, 49, 76
philosopher, 49, 106
philosophy, 2, 7, 41, 85, 126
piece, 120
pioneer, 10, 79, 81
playing, 20
plethora, 23
point, 9, 23, 31, 34, 46, 54
policy, 24
popularity, 111
population, 80, 82, 84
portrayal, 33

position, 94
positive, 27
possibility, 80, 105
potential, 2, 4, 7, 22, 24, 27, 28, 31–34, 39–43, 45, 47, 50–52, 54, 55, 62, 65, 68, 72, 73, 75, 76, 78, 79, 81–86, 92, 95, 97, 100, 102–104, 106, 107, 109, 111–114, 117, 120, 121, 123, 127–129
poverty, 24
power, 12, 14, 16, 21, 23, 31, 41, 60, 68, 75, 79, 80, 125, 128
precipice, 23, 123
precursor, 4
prediction, 23
presence, 34, 73
pressure, 52
principle, 4, 9, 21, 34, 44
print, 20
privacy, 24, 26, 34, 35, 37, 38, 47, 54, 55, 78, 86, 92, 128
problem, 22, 26, 105, 106
procedure, 108
process, 11, 47, 57, 67, 68, 71, 72, 86–88, 95, 120, 123, 126
processing, 44, 49, 57, 60, 71, 72, 75, 95, 111, 126
product, 8
production, 121
productivity, 24, 52, 59, 82, 106
professional, 21, 89
program, 2
programming, 2, 5, 10, 39, 65
progress, 7, 14, 21, 23, 75, 105, 126
project, 4, 7, 89
promise, 18, 33, 46, 85, 115
property, 120

Index

prosody, 69
prospect, 32, 79, 107
public, 20, 26, 27, 33, 35, 47, 59, 83, 95, 113, 115
purpose, 12, 82, 85
pursuit, 50, 52, 60, 83, 85, 103, 113, 129

quality, 14, 19, 20, 39, 70, 75, 82, 102
quest, 5, 7, 62, 79–81, 83, 102, 127, 128
question, 13, 34, 46, 47, 49, 51, 54, 75, 105, 106, 113, 120, 123

rate, 21, 23, 36, 75, 126
Raymond Kurzweil, 3, 12, 23, 31, 43, 60, 62, 79, 81, 83, 85, 123, 125
Raymond Kurzweil's, 1, 5, 7, 8, 10, 12, 14, 17, 19, 33, 58, 59, 61, 65, 68, 70, 76, 97, 121, 123, 126, 128, 130
re, 107
reach, 16, 20, 75, 83
reading, 2, 16, 19, 21, 58, 69
real, 8, 20, 32, 37, 41, 43, 52, 75, 78, 86, 89, 114
realism, 75
reality, 76, 80, 107
realization, 5
realm, 4, 22, 68, 75, 115, 122, 127
recognition, 11–13, 18, 26, 34, 47, 57, 60–62, 72, 78, 85, 95, 97, 126
redefinition, 89
reevaluation, 22, 39, 52
regulation, 26, 32, 35
rehabilitation, 46

relation, 31, 49
relationship, 5, 17, 40, 44, 50, 88, 111, 127, 128
reliance, 92
replication, 2
representation, 5, 71, 121
research, 11, 12, 14, 18, 20, 45, 70, 83–85, 103
resilience, 9, 89
resource, 80, 82, 94
respect, 34
response, 72
responsibility, 23, 35, 52, 115, 121
revolution, 99, 100, 107, 119, 127
rhythm, 69
richness, 52, 53
rift, 84
right, 89
rise, 24, 35, 70, 85, 106
risk, 22, 39, 49, 51, 52, 107, 129
Ritalin, 52
river, 71
road, 105
roadmap, 25
robustness, 18
role, 19, 22, 24, 26, 29, 33, 35, 65, 71, 81, 83, 87–89, 119, 123, 129
rule, 93

safety, 22, 47
Sarah, 20
satisfaction, 95
scenario, 129
school, 10
science, 2, 5, 10, 80, 83, 106
scope, 19
scratch, 2, 4
scrutiny, 32

section, 31, 41, 60, 81, 103, 115, 126
sector, 25, 127
security, 35, 40, 47, 78, 128
selection, 69
self, 18, 22, 50, 76, 94, 105
sense, 18, 20, 49
sentence, 71, 94
sentiment, 95
series, 3, 17
serve, 12, 25, 33, 55, 102, 130
service, 39
set, 10, 12, 70, 71, 75, 126, 128
setting, 2
shape, 1, 10, 12, 31, 48, 50, 55, 75, 77, 80, 124
share, 31
Sherry Turkle, 49
shift, 26, 39, 85, 87, 88, 106, 112
sickness, 76
side, 71
signal, 44, 60, 95, 111
silicon, 105
simulation, 76
singularity, 32, 107
situation, 19, 24
skepticism, 9, 32, 33, 129
skill, 35
skin, 34
society, 14, 20, 22–24, 26–29, 31–33, 38, 41, 51, 53, 55, 59, 80, 82, 84, 85, 107, 110, 129, 130
software, 4, 21, 58
solution, 9
solving, 24, 26, 106
sound, 69
source, 32, 87
speaking, 33
spectrum, 20

speech, 11–14, 20, 21, 68–70, 72, 95–97, 100, 126
speed, 16, 39, 78, 86
spirit, 7, 10, 12
stage, 2, 12, 70, 126, 128
state, 5, 47
status, 22
stem, 80
Stevie Wonder, 8
stewardship, 27
story, 18
structure, 71
struggle, 106
student, 12, 16, 18, 20, 86–88
style, 33
subject, 41
subset, 65
subtraction, 6
success, 14, 20, 67, 85, 90
summary, 10, 19, 25, 80
summer, 2
superintelligence, 24, 32
supply, 39
support, 31, 32, 40, 86, 88, 89
surveillance, 26, 32, 35, 47
sword, 90
syntax, 71, 94
synthesis, 13, 14, 68–70
synthesizer, 8
system, 5, 34, 50, 72

tailor, 85, 88, 127
tandem, 24
tantalizing, 79, 103
tapestry, 1, 43, 121
task, 71
teacher, 87–89, 92
teaching, 72, 88, 127
team, 13, 69

Index

techno, 33
technologist, 12
technology, 1–5, 7–12, 14, 16–24, 26, 31–33, 41, 45–47, 49, 50, 52, 53, 55, 57–62, 65, 68–70, 73–77, 79–81, 83, 85–92, 97, 100, 107, 110, 113, 119, 121, 123, 125–130
telescope, 94
tender, 3, 8
term, 21, 40, 51
territory, 27, 31, 48, 105, 107, 113
test, 54
testament, 10, 14, 16, 72, 83, 130
text, 9, 13, 16, 18, 21, 49, 57–60, 68–70, 72, 95, 100
theory, 3, 85, 126
therapy, 80
thinking, 21, 39, 88, 89
thirst, 10
thought, 2, 44, 46, 49, 50, 122
threat, 35
threshold, 24
thrill, 2
time, 2, 10, 12, 13, 16, 18, 20, 25, 26, 40, 59, 65, 78, 86, 89, 126
today, 59, 72, 97
tool, 18
track, 47
traction, 10, 95
trade, 35
training, 19, 26, 28, 34, 39, 41, 67, 92, 94, 116, 120, 121
trait, 122
trajectory, 23, 25, 126, 130
transcription, 12
transform, 68, 75, 126
transformation, 87

transformer, 94, 95
transhumanism, 41
transition, 24, 26, 40, 106
transparency, 24, 28, 32, 34, 35, 38
treatment, 22, 25, 105
trend, 23, 79, 87
turn, 72
turning, 9

understanding, 2, 4, 5, 7, 9, 12, 23, 31–33, 49–51, 54, 62, 68, 71, 76, 79, 83, 88, 93, 95, 102, 105, 107, 113, 121, 126, 129
undertaking, 31
unemployment, 22, 35, 106
unpredictability, 22
use, 16, 28, 52, 78, 81, 122
user, 9, 50, 70, 72, 75, 78, 95, 120
utilitarianism, 34

value, 9
variability, 62, 69, 93, 96
variety, 13
Vaswani, 94
venture, 12, 50, 105, 115
verb, 72
video, 70
view, 24, 33, 52
vigilance, 36
virtue, 34
vision, 7, 10, 12–14, 22, 32, 58, 60, 62, 70, 76, 77, 97, 102, 105, 123, 127–130
visionary, 5, 21, 25, 31, 83, 126
voice, 60–62, 70, 72
VR, 76
Vygotsky, 86

warfare, 22, 24

water, 84
Watson, 25
way, 8, 9, 12, 13, 20, 21, 53, 59, 61, 65, 70, 81, 95, 100, 105
wealth, 20
well, 34, 85, 88, 125
wellness, 83
whole, 52
will, 19, 22–24, 26, 31, 32, 34, 41, 48, 50, 55, 62, 75–80, 97, 102, 103, 105–107, 121, 125, 129

word, 62, 71
work, 7, 10, 12, 13, 21, 31–33, 39–41, 50, 59, 72, 97, 106, 123, 126, 129
workforce, 39, 40
world, 1–3, 8, 12, 14, 17, 19, 20, 24, 32, 33, 37, 41, 43, 48, 50–52, 59, 76, 79, 89, 92, 114, 123, 125
worth, 52
writing, 2, 49

year, 23

Milton Keynes UK
Ingram Content Group UK Ltd.
UKHW020318021124
450424UK00013B/1321